Paola Gavin was born in Northampton and educated at St. Paul's Girls' School in London. She then studied painting at St. Martin's School of Art. She became a vegetarian in 1965. Two years later she married, and moved with her American actor husband to live in Rome, where she first began to collect vegetarian recipes. Subsequently she has lived in Los Angeles, where she studied screen-writing, Toronto, and Woodstock, New York, where she wrote a food column for the Woodstock Times.

She is currently living with her three daughters in London where she contributes to *The Guardian*, and is in the process of writing another vegetarian cookbook.

'This is an admirable book – clear, practical, and above all, reflecting the rich diversity of Italian vegetable cookery.'
– Matthew Fort, The Guardian.

To Francesca, Bianca and Seana

ITALIAN VEGETARIAN COOKERY

PAOLA GAVIN

ILLUSTRATED BY PETE SMITH

An OPTIMA book

First published in 1987 by
Macdonald Optima

Reprinted and revised in 1991

Reprinted by Optima in 1992

British Library Cataloguing in Publication Data

Gavin, Paola
    Italian vegetarian cookery.
    1. Vegetarian cookery   2. Cookery, Italian
    I. Title
    641.5'63   TX837

    ISBN 0-356-20235 6

Little, Brown and Company (UK) Limited
165 Great Dover Street
London SE1 4YA

Typeset by Leaper & Gard Ltd, Bristol
Printed and bound in Great Britain by
The Guernsey Press Co. Ltd, Guernsey, Channel Islands.

CONTENTS

CONTENTS

INTRODUCTION

The cuisine of Italy has leaned towards vegetarianism for many centuries. In Ancient Rome, the peasants had a basic diet of broth, pasta, vegetables, beans and fruit. During the Renaissance, when Italy looked to Ancient Greece for a rebirth of art and ideas, there was a new interest in vegetarianism – perhaps because Pythagoras and Hippocrates, the founder of modern medicine, were both vegetarians.

Today, Italy is divided into nineteen regions, each of which has its own unique cultural heritage. Over the centuries parts of Italy have been ruled by Etruscans, Romans, Greeks, Saracens, Lombards, Normans, Spaniards, Austrians and many others. Each of these cultures has left its mark, making Italian cooking one of the most varied and exciting in Europe.

Gastronomically, Italy falls into two main categories, partly as a result of simple economics. The more prosperous north uses butter, or a combination of butter and olive oil, as the main cooking fat. There pasta is generally made with eggs, and cattle graze on the rich pastures, making cheese and dairy products plentiful. The south, much of which is poverty stricken, uses olive oil almost exclusively as the main cooking fat. Olive trees grow well on the dry, arid soil and are less expensive to maintain than cattle. Pasta is generally factory-made without eggs. Meat is a luxury, but vegetables are cheap and the growing season extends virtually all the year round. So the diet of the south naturally tends to be vegetarian orientated just as it was in the days of Ancient Rome.

The recipes in this book were collected over the years I was living in Rome and travelling through the regions of Italy. Some were given to me by friends; some I adapted from old Italian cookbooks; many I discovered while travelling and eating in the local *trattorie*. Most of the recipes are very simple to prepare. Italian regional cooking is, after all, a peasant cuisine, a *cucina casalinga* (home-style cooking) that leaves plenty of room for the individual touch (or error)! As Waverley Root writes in *The Food of Italy*, 'while French cooking has become professional cooking even when it is executed by amateurs, Italian cooking has remained basically amateur cooking, even when it is executed by professionals'.

All of these influences add up to a simple, healthy cuisine, based on natural ingredients and using the freshest, seasonal produce. This makes Italy, of all the countries I have ever visited, a veritable vegetarian paradise.

ITALY

THE REGIONS AND THEIR SPECIALITIES

PIEDMONT AND THE VALLE D'AOSTA

Piedmont and the Valle D'Aosta lie in the north-west corner of Italy, backing up against the French and Swiss Alps. The cooking of Piedmont is strongly influenced by the cooking of France (Piedmont was once part of the French Kingdom of Savoy). Piedmont's most famous dish, *fonduta*, is reminiscent of the French and Swiss fondues.

The most prized food of Piedmont is the white truffle, which is found in the hills around Mondavi and the region of Alba. It is usually sliced paper-thin and added very sparingly to enhance the flavour of a dish.

Turin, the elegant capital of Piedmont, is the home of the *grissini* stick, which claims to be the most easily digested form of bread.

Piedmont produces some of the most famous cheese in Italy: Robbiole, Toma and Tomini and, of course, Fontina. Butter and cream are used everywhere for cooking.

This is also polenta and rice country. The Po Valley, which runs through Piedmont, Lombardy and the Veneto, is Italy's main rice-producing region.

The Piedmontese make excellent desserts, especially custards and creams. They are very fond of chocolate. In fact, desserts *alla piemontese* usually mean with chocolate.

Piedmont produces some of the finest wines in Italy: Barolo, Barbera, Freisa, Grignolino, Dolcetto, Barbaresco, Gattinara – which is especially good with rice and truffle dishes, and Nebbiolo. The most famous white wine is the sparkling dessert wine, Asti Spumante. Piedmont is also the major producer of the aperitif, vermouth, which is made from white wine, herbs and spices.

Local specialities

Insalata di fontina Fontina cheese salad with green olives and sweet peppers in a mustard cream dressing.

Insalata di riso alla piemontese Rice salad with asparagus tips, celery, ovoli mushrooms and truffle.

Fonduta Cheese fondue made with eggs, milk, Fontina cheese and truffle.

Asparagi alla zabaione Asparagus served with an egg and wine sauce.

Polenta pasticciata con funghi A layered pie of polenta, mushrooms, Fontina cheese, béchamel sauce and grated cheese.

Polenta in carozza Fried polenta 'sandwiches' filled with Fontina cheese.

Riso in cagnon Rice with melted Fontina cheese.

Risotto al barbera Rice with Barbera wine.

Cisrà Chick pea and turnip soup.

Turta A rice and spinach pie.

Pomodoro ripiene alla novarese Tomatoes stuffed with rice, onions and herbs.

Patate tartufate A potato casserole with cheese and truffles.

Bonet A chocolate almond baked custard.

Pesche ripiene Peaches stuffed with sugar, wine, crushed macaroons and topped with whipped cream.

Ciliege al barolo Cherries cooked in Barolo wine with orange rind and cinnamon.

LOMBARDY

Lombardy is a region of contrasts. It is both the garden of Italy and the most industrialized region in the country, with Milan as its cosmopolitan centre of business. The cooking of Lombardy is so diverse that many of its ancient cities, such as Bergamo, Pavia, Brescia, Como, Cremona and Mantua claim their own cuisines.

The landscape is equally varied, with great Alpine slopes in the north, covered with dense forests and fine mountain pastures, and the breathtaking Italian Lakes, which give way to the rich agricultural plain in the south and the Po Valley.

Rice is the most important crop of the Po Valley. The Milanese eat more rice than they do pasta. Corn is also grown and superb fruit and vegetables. Honey, fruit, walnuts, chestnuts and grapes for wine are produced in the hills to the north. Butter rather than olive oil is the main cooking fat.

Saffron, imported from the Abruzzi region, is a favourite flavouring in Milan. In the Middle Ages alchemists used gold to colour food as they said it cured many ills. Saffron continues this tradition, as it also colours food yellow and is purported to have medicinal properties.

Tomatoes are used sparingly. When they are incorporated into a dish, only enough is added to give a rose colour.

Lombardy produces some of the best cheeses in Italy: Gorgonzola, Bel Paese, Robiolo and Robiolino, Taleggio, the delicate cream cheese Mascarpone, Grana or Parmesan cheese from Lodi and the Italian version of Gruyère cheese, Groviera.

The cooking of Milan is much influenced by Austrian cooking (Lombardy was once part of the Austrian Empire). This is especially noticeable in the love of rich pastries and whipped cream (*lattemiele*). There is also a strong French influence which carries over into the language. Milanese dialect uses the French word *tomate* rather than the Italian *pomodoro*, and *artichaut* for artichoke rather than the Italian *carciofi*.

The best wines of Lombardy come from the Valtellina Region – Sassela, Grumello and Inferno. The famous, slightly bitter aperitif, Campari, is made in Milan.

Local specialities

Asparagi alla lombarda Boiled asparagus served with butter and grated cheese, topped with fried eggs.

Polenta taragna Buckwheat polenta with fresh cheese (*Fiore di latte*).

Polenta pasticciata Polenta layered with béchamel sauce, mushrooms and Gruyère cheese and baked in the oven.

Pizzocheri Buckwheat noodles cooked with potatoes, green beans, cabbage and grated cheese and quickly baked in the oven.

Ris e spargitt Rice with asparagus.

Risotto alla milanese Rice cooked in stock or white wine, saffron, butter and pepper – sometimes topped with sautéed dried mushrooms or truffles.

La risotta A very creamy risotto with onions and saffron.

Tortelli alla cremasca Ravioli stuffed with crushed macaroons, grated cheese, brandy, nutmeg and egg yolks, served with melted butter and grated cheese.

Tortelli di zucca Ravioli stuffed with pumpkin, eggs, crushed macaroons, Verona mustard (more a chutney than a mustard), candied citron, served with sage butter and grated cheese.

Scarpazza A spinach or cabbage tart.

Minestrone alla milanese A very thick vegetable soup thickened with rice – never pasta. It may be served cold in the summer.

Zuppa pavese A soup of stock, eggs, fried bread and grated cheese – a speciality of Pavia.

Broccoli alla milanese Boiled broccoli dipped in cheese-flavoured eggs then in breadcrumbs and fried in butter.

Mozzarella milanese A misnomer; Bel Paese is always used, dipped in flour then egg and breadcrumbs, and deep-fried.

Torta del paradiso A very light and delicate cake flavoured with vanilla and lemon rind.

Pannetone The traditional Italian Christmas cake – a simple cake, similar to a brioche, with raisins, candied peel and citron.

Crema di mascarpone Mascarpone cream cheese mixed with rum, sugar, egg yolks and cinnamon.

Torrone Nougat made with honey, almonds, egg white and candied peel – a speciality of Cremona.

TRENTINO AND ALTO ADIGE

The Alto Adige belonged to Austria until the First World War when, under the Treaty of Versailles, it was given to Italy. The landscape is spectacular. Here lies the majestic Marmallada, the highest mountain in the Dolomites. The valleys spilling into the Adige River are very fertile – rye, wheat, maize, oats and barley are cultivated. Vines and fruit trees are grown on the hillsides and it is the only region of Italy that cultivates raspberries.

The vegetables grown are simple and Teutonic in character: red and white cabbages, potatoes, turnips and kohlrabi. The *trattorie* serve German-sounding dishes: *knödeln* and *canederli* for gnocchi; *schwammerlsuppe* is a cream of mushroom soup; *riebl* is a fritter made of buckwheat flour.

The local breads are often heavy and made of mixed grains, like the rye bread of Merano and *brazadel.* They are often flavoured with caraway seeds – once believed to be an aphrodisiac.

There is a fondness for pastries and sweets which reflects their Austro-Hungarian roots. Excellent strudels are made, filled with apples, pears, cherries or soured cream (*rahmstrudel*), as are fruit-filled pancakes (*schmarren*) and fritters (*fritelle*).

The wines of the region are excellent. The most noted white wines are Termeno, which is particularly good with antipasti and egg dishes, Riesling and Terlano, which is excellent with minestrone and bean soups. Santa Maddalena, Teroldego and Lagreinkretzer are also superior red wines.

Local specialities
Zuppa di farina abbrustolita A potato and milk soup thickened with flour.

Schwammerlsuppe Cream of mushroom soup.

Zwiebelsuppe A gruel-like onion soup flavoured with sugar and vinegar.

Mus A cornmeal and wheat milk soup, the consistency of porridge.

Gnocchi tirolesi neri Buckwheat and rye flour gnocchi.

Türteln Rye flour ravioli, stuffed with cabbage or sauerkraut, flavoured with onion, caraway seeds, chives and marjoram.

Frittata alla trentina A fluffy omelette. It may be served with tomato, mushroom or cheese filling.

Erdbeertorte Raspberry tart.

Presnitz A pastry with an elaborate filling of almonds, walnuts, breadcrumbs, butter, sugar, sultanas, chocolate, lemon rind, citron, rum and vanilla.

Krapfen Doughnuts.

Pane tirolesi A slightly sweet bread flavoured with almonds, lemon and cinnamon.

VENETO

The cooking of the Veneto or Venezia Euganea is one of the most elegant in Italy. The city of Venice, with its ornate palaces lining the famous Grand Canal, is a constant reminder that it was the most affluent city in Europe in the Middle Ages. Its wealth came from the spice trade with Constantinople and the Orient. It was to Venice that sugar, pepper, nutmeg, cloves, ginger and coffee were first brought, and then distributed around Europe.

The Veneto region includes the ancient cities of Vicenza, Padua, Treviso and Verona (immortalized by Romeo and Juliet), the eastern shore of Lake Garda, and a portion of the Dolomiti Mountains in the north with the famous ski resort of Cortina D'Ampezzo.

Artichokes, peas, cabbages, courgettes, pumpkins, onions, tomatoes and the famous asparagus of Bassano are cultivated in the southerly plains. Mushrooms, peaches and wine grapes are grown in the hills. Rice, grown in the Po Valley, is eaten more than pasta in the Veneto region and it is served with an enormous variety of vegetables. The most famous rice dish is *risi e bisi* (rice with peas), using the tiniest, most tender, sweetest peas found in May and June.

The town of Treviso, with its canals and delightful market, is famous for *radicchio rosso* or red endive, which is grown nowhere else in Italy. The best beans in Italy are from Lamon, in the Province of Belluno, where, of course, bean soups are often served.

The Veneto region is celebrated for its cakes and pastries, many of which include cornmeal. Three cheeses are produced in the region: Asiago, made near Vicenza; Ricotta; and Casatella, a soft buttery cheese made from cow's milk.

The wines of the Veneto are superior. The most well known are Soave, Valpolicella, Bardolino, Garganega, Prosecco and Tocai. Tocai, Soave and Valpolicella are all especially good with pasta.

Local specialities

Risi e bisi Rice and peas.
Risi e fasoi Rice and beans.
Risi e cavoli Rice, cauliflower, onion, garlic, butter, oil and sage.
Risi e zucca Rice and pumpkin cooked in butter and milk.
Risi e porri Rice with leeks.

Riso co' la ua Rice with Malaga grapes and, sometimes, pine nuts.

Risi con fenoci Rice with fennel.

Bigoli con le noci Wholewheat noodles with walnut sauce.

Gnocchi padovani Potato gnocchi made with buckwheat flour.

Gnocchi alla veronese Potato gnocchi served with sugar, cinnamon and grated cheese.

Polenta fasola Polenta with beans.

Colomba di pasqua An Easter cake flavoured with cloves, cinnamon, almonds, Kirsch and orange rind.

Pandoro veronese A dome-shaped cake flavoured with rum and vanilla.

Torta saviosa A cake made with cornmeal, potato flour, butter, vanilla, sugar, eggs and aniseed.

Torta di zucca Pumpkin cake.

Cotinfe A simple dessert made of dried apples, honey and wine.

FRIULI AND VENEZIA GIULIA

Friuli and Venezia Giulia lie in the north-east of Italy, bordering on Yugoslavia and Austria. The region is largely mountainous and not very fertile. Maize, root vegetables, artichokes and asparagus are grown in the Friuli plain.

This is the poorest region in northern Italy. Bread and vegetables are the mainstay of the diet. Vegetable *frittate* (omelettes) are popular and are known by strange dialect names – *Fertae cu lis jerbúzzis* is a mixed herb omelette that includes nasturtium leaves.

Many of the rice dishes of the Veneto region are also found here. Montasio cheese, somewhat similar to Emmenthal, is made in the province of Udine.

This is wine country. Some of the names are confusing, as they are the same as many of the wines from the Trentino and Alto Adige. Tocai, Riesling, Traminer, Sauvignon, Pino Bianco are fine white wines, and Merlot,

Cabernet Franc and Pinot Nero was the best-known red wines.

Local specialities
Fricco Fresh cheese and apples cooked with butter, served as an antipasto.

Minestra di riso alia friuliana Rice soup with egg, lemon and grated cheese.

Iota Bean and sauerkraut soup.

Paparot A thick soup of cornmeal and spinach.

Sopa friuliana Celery soup, traditionally served on Christmas Eve.

Ciarscons alla carniola Ravioli stuffed with Ricotta cheese, raisins, parsley, breadcrumbs and spices.

Fertae cui cesarons Frittata (omelette) made with onions, leeks, peas and fennel.

Fritole di fenoci Fennel fritters.

Zastoch French bean, potato and pumpkin stew.

Brovada Marinated turnips fried in olive oil and garlic and flavoured with caraway seeds.

Gubana A sweet pastry with sultanas, walnuts, pine nuts, prunes, dried figs, crystallized orange rind and bitter chocolate.

LIGURIA

Liguria is the narrow coastal region hugging the Gulf of Genoa in the north-west. It stretches from the French frontier in the west to La Spezia and the border of Tuscany in the east. It is largely mountainous with a spectacular coast road tunnelling through terraced hill-sides that drop precipitously down to the blue sea below. This is the Italian Riviera with such famous resort towns as San Remo, Portofino and Santa Margherita.

The main city is Genoa, which rivals Bologna as the gastronomic capital of Italy. Genoa is famous for its green basil sauce *pesto* which is lavished on pasta and in soups.

The whole region abounds with fresh fruit and

vegetables – especially green vegetables and herbs of all kinds: marjoram, oregano, parsley, bay leaf, sage, fennel, rosemary, walnuts, pine nuts, olives and capers are all in constant use.

The cuisine of Liguria excels in its vegetable cookery. Vegetable tarts, gratins and stuffed vegetables of all kinds are made.

Very little cheese is made in Liguria except Ricotta, which is made in Savona. The most common cheese used is Pecorino Sardo, which is imported from Sardinia.

The Ligurians, like their French neighbours, are fond of sweet pastries and candied fruits, especially *marrons glacés* (crystallized chestnuts).

Liguria produces few wines. The most notable are the dry rosé Dolceaqua and the white wine from the villages of the Cinqueterre, near La Spezia.

Local specialities

Pesto alla genovese A sauce of fresh basil, olive oil, Pecorino Sardo cheese and pine nuts.

Condijon A mixed salad with onion, pepper, tomato, olives and capers.

Sardenaira A pizza topped with onions, black olives, capers, garlic and marjoram.

La torta pasqualina Literally this means 'Easter Tart' and is a speciality of Genoa. Paper-thin sheets of pastry are filled with spinach, Ricotta cheese, eggs and herbs. Artichokes are sometimes substituted for spinach.

La torta di funghi e zucchini Similar to *la torta pasqualina*, but with a filling of mushrooms, courgettes, Ricotta cheese, eggs and herbs.

Trenette col pesto Ribbon noodles cooked with potatoes and tiny French beans.

Minestrone alla genovese A thick vegetable soup flavoured with pesto sauce.

Preboggion Rice and herb soup flavoured with pesto sauce.

Frittate di bietole Swiss chard omelette with onion, grated cheese and oregano.

Taggien verdi Green noodles made with Swiss chard, spinach and borage, served with mushroom sauce and grated cheese.
Troffie alla genovese Potato gnocchi served with butter, pesto sauce and grated cheese.
Polpettone di fagiolini A French bean and potato pie.
Foccaccia alla salvia Sage flat bread.
Pane dolce 'Sweet bread', with sultanas, pine nuts and candied fruit – a speciality of Genoa.

TUSCANY

Tuscany is one of the largest regions of Italy. Although not quite the geographic centre, to many Italians it is the heart of Italy. Certainly it was the heart of the Renaissance.

It is hard not to talk in superlatives when speaking of Tuscany. It has produced some of the greatest artists, writers and thinkers of all time: Michelangelo, Leonardo da Vinci, Piero della Francesca, Botticelli, Fra Angelico, Giotto, Boccaccio and Galileo, to name just a few. Some of the most beautiful towns in Italy are found here: Florence, Siena, Lucca, Arezzo, San Gimignano and Pisa.

Tuscan speech is the purest form of Italian. The countryside, mainly gently rolling hills covered with olive groves, vineyards and pastures, is both peaceful and inspiring. It has a long coastline of white sandy beaches. Many a passing traveller has fallen under its spell and stayed a lifetime.

The Tuscans have a distaste for excess, inherited perhaps from their Etruscan ancestors. Tuscans are simple and refined and so is their cooking, which relies upon the combination of the finest ingredients and the artistry of their cooks. Few sauces and garnishes disguise the natural flavour of the food. They are masters of vegetable cookery, especially of the haricot bean, brought from America in the sixteenth century. Tuscans are so fond of beans that a Tuscan is often referred to in other parts of the country as a *mangiafagioli* or 'bean-eater'. They also rival the Romans in the cooking of artichokes. The best olive oil is purported to come from Lucca, although most Tuscans use luscious green olive oil from olives grown and pressed in their local villages. Butter is often combined with olive oil in cooking.

The most famous wine of Tuscany is Chianti, of which there are many grades – Chianti Classico is always of top quality. Montepulciano is another fine local red wine, as is Carmignano and the sweet dessert wine from Elba, Aleatico di Portferraio.

Local specialities
Acquacotta 'Cooked water', a vegetable broth with onions, celery and tomatoes, poured over eggs, cheese and bread.
La cipollata An onion soup.
L'infarinata A vegetable soup thickened with cornmeal.
Zuppa di fagioli A thick bean soup poured over toast.
La ribollita Zuppa di fagioli, cooled and reheated (reboiled) with more olive oil and gratinéed in the oven.
La fette A black cabbage (*cavolo neri*) soup.
Strozzapreti alla fiorentina Spinach and Ricotta gnocchi.
Striche e ceci Noodles and chick peas flavoured with garlic, olive oil and rosemary.
Risotto alla toscana A summer risotto with tomato, courgettes, peas and asparagus tips.
Asparagi alla toscana Boiled asparagus sautéed in butter, topped with grated cheese and fried eggs.
Tortino di carciofi A baked artichoke omelette.
Fagioli al fiasco Dried white beans cooked in a wine flask with olive oil, garlic and sage.
Fagioli all' uccelletto Boiled dried white beans cooked with olive oil, garlic, sage and tomato purée.
Castagnaccio A pizza or flat cake made of chestnut flour topped with raisins, pine nuts and fennel seeds.
Cenci alla fiorentina Ribbons of dough tied in bows, then fried in oil and dusted with sugar.
Panforte di siena A rich fruit-cake made with almonds,

walnuts, crystallized watermelon and orange rind, sugar, flour and spices.

Ricciarelli di siena Almond macaroons.

EMILIA-ROMAGNA

Emilia-Romagna is bounded by the Po River in the north, the Adriatic Sea in the east and the Apennini Mountains in the south and west. It consists mainly of a rich, fertile plain, dotted with some of the most ancient towns in Italy – Piacenza, Parma, Bologna, Ferrara, Modena and Ravenna.

Bologna, city of medieval arcades and towers (two of which seem to lean over as much as the famous leaning Tower of Pisa), is nicknamed *La Grassa* or 'fat one' due to its rich and fattening cuisine. Many Italians consider Bologna the gastronomic capital of Italy.

Fruits and vegetables are grown in abundance, especially table grapes, apples, pears, peaches, strawberries, tomatoes, sugar beets, asparagus, potatoes, courgettes and almonds. Wheat is also cultivated. Emilia-Romagna is famous for its pasta – lasagne is said to have been invented here.

Butter and olive oil are both used in cooking. The creamy butter of the region (*burro di panna*) is much sought after in the rest of Italy.

Perhaps the most famous product of Emilia-Romagna is Parmesan cheese, or *parmigiano reggiana*, as it is called in Italy. The cheese is made in the regions of Parma, Reggio Nell'Emigla and Modena. All other Parmesan cheese made outside this controlled region is called *Grana.*

Lambrusco is the best-known wine of Emilia-Romagna, but it does not travel well. Sangiovese and Vino Rosso del Bosco are two wines worthy of note. Several good liqueurs are distilled here, including Nocino (made from walnuts), Sassolino (made from star anise imported from China), Rosolio and various fruit-flavoured brandies.

Local specialities

Passatelli in brodo Spinach dumplings in broth.

Tortelle d'erbette Ring-shaped ravioli stuffed with spinach and herbs.

Capellacci con la zucca Ravioli with pumpkin stuffing – a speciality of Ferrara.

Tortei con la cua Butterfly-shaped ravioli stuffed with Ricotta cheese and herbs.

Tagliatelle alla salsa di noci Noodles with Ricotta cheese, butter, grated cheese and crushed walnuts.

Ravioli con formaggio Ravioli stuffed with cottage cheese, cinnamon, nutmeg, cloves and saffron – a speciality of Faenza.

Asparagi alla parmigiana Boiled asparagus topped with butter and grated cheese and baked in the oven.

Carciofi alla parmigiana Boiled artichoke hearts in cream sauce topped with grated cheese and baked in the oven.

Erbazzone dolce A sweet Swiss chard pie with Ricotta cheese, sugar, almonds, rum and lemon rind.

Pampepato di cioccolato A chocolate cake made with honey, milk, almonds, lemon rind, pepper and spices.

Frittate dolce di pignoli Sweet pine nut fritters flambéed in rum.

Amaretti Macaroons.

La bonissimma A light cake, flavoured with vanilla and lemon, with a filling of honey, rum, crushed walnuts and chocolate.

UMBRIA

Like Lombardy, Umbria has no coastline. It has several lakes, the largest being Lake Trasimeno. The landscape, with its rolling hills and ancient hill towns, is that of medieval paintings come to life. Here is Assisi, birthplace of St Francis, as well as Gubbio, Spoleto and Perugia – a delightful citadel – perched on a mountain ridge surrounded by Roman walls and Etruscan ramparts.

The valleys are often steep but fertile, with sheep

grazing on the hills. In the lowlands, wheat, vegetables, olives and fruit are grown. Plums and figs are dried for export. Many varieties of mushrooms are grown; the best-known are the black truffles of Norcia and Spoleto. The Romans believed them to be an aphrodisiac. There is an old saying that goes: 'Those who wish to lead virtuous lives should abstain from eating truffles.'

Perugia has a sweet tooth. The streets and alleys are filled with pastry shops. The famous Perugina chocolates are made here.

Umbria is not known for its cheeses but two cheeses are produced: Caciotto, made from cow's milk, and Pecorino cheese.

Orvieto is unrivalled as the best wine of Umbria. Dry, white and pleasing, it has been a favourite of cardinals and painters for centuries. Orvieto also makes a fine Vino Santo.

Local specialities

Cipollata Onion soup with tomato, thickened with egg.

Spaghetti all aglio e olio Spaghetti with garlic, olive oil and hot pepper.

Ciriole ternane Noodles with a tomato and mushroom sauce.

Spaghetti alla noci Spaghetti with a sauce of walnuts, pine nuts and garlic.

Strangozzi di Spoleto Ribbon noodles with tomato sauce, herbs and garlic.

Frittata di tartufi Truffle omelette.

Sedani di trevi in umido Fresh celery in tomato sauce.

Torta col formaggio Cheesecake.

Cicerchiata 'Chick peas' or nuts of dough deep-fried, coated with boiling honey and left to set.

Pestringolo A very rich fruit cake made of dried figs, raisins, almonds, pine nuts, candied peel, breadcrumbs, cocoa, honey and spices.

Pinnochiate Crystallized pine nuts, flavoured with orange and lemon rind.

LE MARCHE

The Marches, or Le Marche, as it is called by the Italians, is a lesser-known region of Italy. It consists of rolling hills, descending from the Apennini ridge of mountains in the west to the Adriatic Sea in the east. The coastline is dotted with a handful of fishing villages and several small resort towns, including Pesaro and Senigallia, more popular with Italian tourists than the more sophisticated foreigner. Ancona, the capital of the Marches, is the main seaport of the central Adriatic. Unfortunately, much of the old town was destroyed in the two world wars.

The Marches is largely agricultural. Vegetables, fruit trees, olives, wine grapes and wheat are grown, and sheep and goats graze on the hillsides.

The most outstanding town in the region is the graceful hill town of Urbino, with its fine Ducal palace built by one of the greatest patrons of the Renaissance, Federigo da Montrefeltro.

The only well-known wine of the region is the bright, straw-coloured Verdicchio dei Castelli di Jesi. Vino Santo is made in Urbino.

Local specialities

Minestra di ceci Chick pea soup thickened with corn meal.
Pisselata alla maceratese Pea soup with onion, tomato, garlic and herbs.
Zuppa di fagioli all' anconetana Bean soup cooked with garlic, celery, parsley and hot red pepper.
Crocchette di uova alla marchigiana Egg croquettes.
Calcioni (Ravioli all' ascolana) Ravioli stuffed with fresh Pecorino cheese, egg yolks, sugar, lemon and grated cheese, topped with grated cheese and oil and baked in the oven.
Risotto alla rossini Rice with egg and mushrooms.
Pizza al formaggio Cheese bread made with Parmesan, Pecorino and Gruyère cheeses.
Fave alla compagnola Broad beans served with onion sauce.

Frittata co' la minduccia omelette flavoured with mint.
Ciambelle col mosto A ring-shaped cake flavoured with wine.
Bostrenge A chocolate rice pudding.

ROME AND THE LAZIO

Rome dominates the cooking of the Lazio. It combines the cooking of the north with that of the south. It is a simple but robust cuisine, not unlike the cooking of Tuscany.

The streets of Rome abound with restaurants and *trattorie*, especially in the charming Trastevere quarter. Eating out in Rome is a way of life. It has earned its nickname 'City of a Thousand Meals'.

The Lazio is wine and olive country. Vegetables, especially broccoli, peas, fennel, artichokes and tomatoes, grow well in the countryside around Rome, as can be seen by the abundant produce at the famous Campo dei Fiori market in Old Rome.

Mint is a characteristic flavour of Roman cooking, and vegetables are often dressed simply with garlic, olive oil and vinegar (*all'agro*).

The Lazio is famous for its Pecorino Romano and Ricotta cheeses. They have been made here for more than two thousand years. Provatura, Caciocavallo and Mozzarella cheeses are also produced.

Frascati, one of the wines of the Castelli Romani Hills, is the favourite wine of the Romans. Unfortunately, it does not travel well. Colli Albani is another dry white wine from the same region. Est! Est! Est! di Montefiascone (literally meaning 'big flask', an appropriate name) is probably the most celebrated wine of the Lazio and excellent served with pasta.

A Roman meal is not complete without a glass of the famous anisette liqueur, Sambuca. Ask for it *con le mosche* (literally 'with flies'), which, in fact, are coffee beans which you crunch while sipping the liqueur.

Local specialities

Cipolline in agrodolce Onions cooked in a sweet and sour sauce with tomatoes.

Carciofi alla romana Artichokes stewed in olive oil, garlic and mint.

Carciofi alla giudea Deep-fried artichokes.

Stracciatella Egg drop soup.

Gnocchi alla romana Semolina gnocchi baked with butter and grated cheese.

Fettucine con la ricotta Egg noodles with Ricotta and unsalted butter.

Fettucine al burro Egg noodles with butter and cheese.

Spaghetti alla marinara Spaghetti with a sauce of tomatoes, garlic, olive oil and hot pepper.

Insalata di misticanza A salad of wild greens and herbs, including rocket, sorrel, mint, lamb's lettuce, chicory and purslane.

Bietole strascinati Beet leaves or Swiss chard sautéed with garlic and olive oil.

Spinaci alla romana Spinach cooked with olive oil, pine nuts and raisins.

Supplì al telefono Rice croquettes stuffed with Provatura cheese.

Torta di ricotta A Ricotta cheesecake with lemon rind, vanilla, sugar and liqueur.

Zuppa inglese Literally 'English soup' – a rum-soaked cake topped with custard.

ABRUZZI AND MOLISE

The Abruzzi and Molise is mountain country, stretching from the Adriatic Sea in the east to some of the highest peaks in the Italian peninsula. The region is wild and rocky with some of the most imposing scenery in Italy. Wild bears and wolves still roam in the Abruzzi National Park near Scanno.

Sheep and cattle graze on the high mountain pastures. Scamorza cheese, made from cow's milk, is the most commonly produced cheese, but Caciocavallo, Pecorino, Provola and Ricotta are also made. Cheese is used considerably in the cooking of the region.

Like the landscape, the cuisine is simple and stark. There is a strong liking for hot red peppers (*peperoncini*), which flavour many of the local dishes.

The most famous pasta speciality is *Maccheroni alla chitarra*. These are home-made noodles, cut on a chitarra or wooden frame with steel strings strung across it like a guitar. The noodles are laid over the strings and pressed through so they fall into long thin strands. Most homes in the Abruzzi own a chitarra.

The Abruzzi is the only region of Italy where saffron is grown, although it is seldom used in the local cooking, but instead is exported to Lombardy in the north.

The rocky landscape is not well suited to the cultivation of grapes but a few local wines are produced: Cerasuolo d'Abruzzo, a clear red wine that goes well with Scamorza cheese, soups and vegetables; and Montepulciano d'Abruzzo (red) and Trebbiano d'Abruzzo (white).

Local specialities
Zuppa di cardi Cardoon soup.

Timballo di melanzane A layered pie of fried aubergine, Scamorza cheese and beaten egg.

Ceci di navelli Chick peas cooked with onion, olive oil and rosemary, served with cubes of fried bread.

Cardoni fritti all' abruzzese Cardoon fritters.

Scripelle 'mbusse Pancakes usually stuffed with peas, Pecorino cheese and a white sauce, topped with a tomato and mushroom sauce and baked in the oven.

Frittate con le patate Omelette with potatoes, onions and hot peppers.

Maccheroni con agli, olio e diavolillio Macaroni with garlic, olive oil, parsley and hot peppers.

Ravioli all' aquilana Cheese-stuffed ravioli, served with sage butter and grated Pecorino cheese.

Parozzo A light cake made with cornflour or potato flour with ground almonds, butter, eggs and sugar with a chocolate frosting.

Pepatelli Biscuits made with wholemeal flour, honey, chopped almonds, grated orange rind and pepper.

CAMPANIA

Campania is, perhaps, the most beautiful of all the regions of Italy. It is hard to surpass the majesty of the azure Bay of Naples, dominated by Mount Vesuvius, or the magnificent Amalfi drive with its white Saracen villages set like jewels along its stony cliffs. No wonder that it has been the playground of travellers, artists, poets and aristocrats for decades. In contrast, Naples, the second largest port in Italy, is vibrant, noisy, overcrowded and marked by poverty.

Campania is mainly agricultural. A profusion of fruits and vegetables have been grown on the rich volcanic soil since Roman times. The growing season extends virtually all the year round. Courgettes, aubergines, tomatoes, green beans, cabbage, broccoli, melons, cherries, figs, apples, pears, citrus fruit, grapes, olives, almonds, walnuts and chestnuts are all cultivated. Some of the most delectable vegetable dishes in Italy are made here.

Naples is most famous for pizza, which literally means 'pie.' Pizza was made two thousand years ago in Pompeii without tomatoes, of course, which were not introduced to Italy until the sixteenth century.

Naples is also renowned for its macaroni which it has been manufacturing since the fifteenth century. It is served with colourful and piquant sauces. All over Italy *alla Napoletana* means 'with a rich tomato sauce'.

Mozzarella cheese is made in the region of Naples. Once it was only made with buffalo's milk, but today a large amount is made with cow's milk, as the buffalo now graze on more inland pastures. Provola, Provolone, Caciocavallo and Ricotta are also made here.

Several wines of note are produced in the Naples area. The red Gragnano is the Neapolitans' favourite. Falerno and Lacrima Christi are the most famous wines of the region. Ravello and Capri both produce pleasing dry white wines.

Local specialities

Minestra di zucchine Courgette soup.

Insalata di rinforzo Boiled cauliflower with vinaigrette dressing, topped with black olives and capers.

Melanzane alla parmigiana Fried aubergine layered with tomato sauce and Mozzarella cheese and baked in the oven.

Patate alla pizzaiola Sliced boiled potatoes fried in olive oil with garlic, tomatoes and herbs.

Pizza margherita A classic pizza topped with tomatoes, Mozzarella cheese and herbs.

Calzone A stuffed pizza in the shape of a 'trouser leg'.

Mozzarella al ferri Grilled Mozzarella cheese.

Mozzarella in carrozza Mozzarella cheese sandwiched between slices of bread and fried in hot oil.

Crespolini al formaggio Cheese-filled pancakes.

Linguine alla puttanesca Linguine with a sauce of tomatoes, black olives, capers, garlic and hot pepper.

Strangulaprievete Literally 'priest strangler', potato

dumplings with tomato sauce.

Macaroni alla caprese Macaroni with Fior di Latte cheese, fried aubergine, tomatoes, garlic and basil.

Pastiera A rich puff pastry filled with grains of wheat boiled in milk, Ricotta cheese and candied fruits, flavoured with orange flower water and cinnamon.

Zeppole alla napoletana Marsala-flavoured fritters.

BASILICATA

Basilicata (or Lucania, as it is sometimes called) is the least visited region of Italy and the poorest. It has two short stretches of coastline, one to the west overlooking the Tyrrhenian Sea tucked between Campania and Calabria, the other on the instep of Italy along the Ionian Sea between Calabria and Apulia.

The terrain is wild and almost totally mountainous. The two main cities are Potenza, which is almost vertical, and Matera, an awesome city hugging the slopes of two ravines, with its hodge-podge of houses and ancient cave dwellings hewn out of the rock face.

Despite the harshness of the land, wheat, vegetables and fruit, especially citrus fruit, figs, walnuts, chestnuts, olives and wine grapes, are grown wherever possible.

The cooking of Basilicata is simple and austere, based on pasta, vegetables and legumes, with plenty of garlic, hot peppers, olives and capers. The people like their food hot – chilli pepper is used to spice everything from tomato sauce to fried eggs.

Several cheeses are produced – a sharp Provolone, Caciocavallo, Scamorza, Mozzarella, Ricotta and Ricotta Salata, a small hard goat cheese called Casiddi and the semi-soft Manteca.

The only wine of note is the dry red Aglianico del Vulture, which claims to be the best wine of southern Italy.

Local specialities

Cicoria e favette A purée of dried beans served with a salad of cooked greens and bread – a speciality of Matera.
Laàn Tagliatelle with lentils or dried beans.
Maccheroni alla trainera Macaroni with olive oil, capers, garlic and ginger.
Lasagne con pangrattato fritto Lasagne with fried bread-crumbs.
Lagane e ceci A kind of tagliatelle served with chick peas, olive oil, garlic and hot red pepper.
Mandorlata di peperoni Sweet and sour peppers with almonds and raisins.
Mostaccioli A primitive biscuit made with flour and honey.
Manate A pasta dish made entirely of one long strand of fresh spaghetti.
Cuccia A sweet made with walnuts, pomegranate seeds and honey.
Pettole A sweet fritter.

CALABRIA

Calabria, when it was under Greek rule 2500 years ago, was the richest region of Italy. The main city was Sybaris, near the Gulf of Taranto, which later gave its name to the English language to mean the 'epitome of luxury' (and sometimes, degeneracy). Sybaris has disappeared without a trace, but Calabria has more Greek ruins than any other region of Italy.

Today, Calabria is a region plagued by earthquakes and poverty. Its coastline is spectacular and has opened up to tourism in recent years. Most of the land is harsh and mountainous; the water resources are meagre; unemployment is rampant. Many of the young men have been forced to seek employment abroad in order to support their families.

The cooking of Calabria, like its neighbour Campania, is based on pasta, legumes and vegetables, but it is more strongly flavoured with chilli peppers, olives, oregano and mint. Aubergines, peppers, tomatoes, courgettes, artichokes, olives, almonds, citrus fruits, figs and grapes are grown on the more fertile slopes and in the valleys. Delicious vegetables soups, pies and *pitte*, stuffed and baked vegetables and a wide variety of sweet pastries made with honey and nuts are prepared.

Several cheeses are made: Caciocavallo, Pecorino, Mozzarella, fresh Ricotta and Ricotta Salata.

Calabrian wines tend to be heavy and strong, and many are used for blending with the subtler wines of northern Italy.

Local specialities
Licurdia An onion and potato soup flavoured with hot pepper and served with croûtons – a speciality of Cosenza.
Millecosedde A very thick minestrone soup made with a wide variety of dried and fresh vegetables.
Maccheroni alla pastora Literally 'shepherd's macaroni', this is served with fresh Ricotta cheese, butter and salt.
Maccheroni con carciofi Macaroni with artichokes.
Pasta asciutta alla callabrese Pasta with tomato sauce and strongly flavoured with chilli pepper.
Melanzane all 'agrodolce Fried aubergines topped with a sweet and sour sauce of vinegar, sugar, cinnamon, walnuts, raisins, candied peel, Marsala and chocolate.
Gianfottere A vegetable stew of aubergines, courgettes, tomatoes, potatoes, onions, herbs and saffron.
Rigatoncelli con pomodori Tomatoes stuffed with pasta, flavoured with parsley, mint, garlic and olive oil.
Turiddu A biscuit made of flour, eggs and almonds.
Nepitelle Crescent-shaped pastries filled with walnuts, almonds, dried figs, raisins, candied orange peel and spices.
Crocette Figs stuffed with almonds and fennel seeds and lightly roasted in the oven.

APULIA

Apulia is the spur and heel of the Italian boot, stretching from the Gargano Peninsula, down the Adriatic coast to the Ionian Sea. The sun-drenched, whitewashed, cubist towns along the coast are more reminiscent of Greece than Italy.

It is an isolated region, steeped in ancient history, with the remains of a Doric temple at Taranto, the bronze colossus at Barletta, the strange conical roofed *trulli* of Alberobello, and the Norman castle of Castel del Monte, near the town of Andria.

Although Apulia is the richest of the three most southerly regions of Italy, it is still very poor. The northern plains, once providing pasture land for vast herds of sheep, are now mainly used for market gardening. Potatoes, aubergines, artichokes, fennel, broad beans, asparagus, melons and citrus fruits are all cultivated. The region around Bari produces more wheat, olives and wine than any other region of Italy.

The cooking of Apulia is very basic. Bread is the most important staple. Like most of southern Italy, the diet is based on pasta and vegetables. Onions are used more than garlic in cooking, and green vegetables of all kinds are used to stuff pies and *calzoni*, or as an accompaniment to pasta. Many cultivated and wild herbs are used, as well as plenty of chilli peppers, black and green olives and capers.

A wide selection of local cheeses are made: Cariotta, a whey cheese made in Brindisi; Ricotta; Mozzarella (called Provalina in Bari); Scamorza; and Burrata (which has a butter filling).

Like Calabria, Apulian wines are strong and used for blending with the wines of the north. The best known is probably the white wine of San Severo. Several dessert wines with a high alcoholic content are produced.

Local specialities
Frisa A wholewheat bun soaked with olive oil and spread with onion and tomato.
La capriata A bean purée flavoured with olive oil and onions, usually served with a salad of cooked greens.
Minestrone verde alla barese A thick green vegetable soup, including turnip tops, Swiss chard, fennel, curly endive and, sometimes, cardoons.
Pizza rustica alla leccese A double-crust pie made of yeast

dough or shortcrust pastry. It may have a cheese, tomato or onion filling.

Calzone alla barese A stuffed pizza in the shape of a 'trouser leg', filled with sautéed greens, tomatoes and cheese.

Panzerotti con ricotta alla barese Deep-fried ravioli stuffed with egg and Ricotta cheese.

Orecchiette con cime di rape Pasta in the shape of 'little ears' served with turnip tops and chilli pepper.

Simmuledda alla foggiana Potato and fennel soup, thickened with cornmeal.

Tiella A layered pie of potatoes, onions, vegetables and herbs, sometimes including rice.

Taranto tart A flat pie of mashed potatoes, topped with Mozzarella cheese and tomatoes and baked in the oven.

Melanzane alla foggiana Stuffed aubergines with olive oil, garlic, tomatoes, breadcrumbs and herbs.

Fritto di melanzane filanti Fried aubergine and cheese sandwiches.

Carteddate Wine-flavoured pastries coated with honey.

SICILY

The island of Sicily is Mediterranean in the north and sub-tropical in the centre and south. The usual Mediterranean vegetables and fruits are grown: artichokes, aubergines, courgettes, tomatoes, broccoli, peppers, fennel, olives and capers. The largest amount of citrus fruit in all Italy is grown in Sicily, as well as grapes, Smyrna figs and such exotic fruits as pomegranates, prickly pears, loquats and Japanese medlars. Sicily also produces a large amount of wheat. In fact, it has had a wheat surplus for two thousand years. No wonder the staples of the poor are bread and macaroni.

The cooking of Sicily is spicy and full of flavour. It is characteristic of Sicilian cooking to have a multiplicity of tastes in one dish. Sicilian food has some surprises: a taste of chocolate in a sweet and sour aubergine dish, or a hint

of sultanas in a fritter of chopped olives. It is a cuisine much influenced by the Arabs, which is especially reflected in the pastries and sweets as they include honey, sesame seeds, almonds, pistachio nuts and aniseed.

Sicily produces several cheeses, mainly from ewe's milk. These include Incanestrato, Caciocavallo (often used for grating when aged), Pepato and Ricotta Salata.

Although Sicilian wine is often considered coarser than the wines of northern Italy, there are some fine wines to be found including Corvo (white and red) and Faro (red). The best-known wine is, of course, Marsala, which may be drunk as an aperitif or a dessert wine. Malvasia di Lipari is another noted dessert wine.

Local specialities
Maccu A broad bean soup or purée flavoured with wild fennel and peperoncini.
La caponata Fried aubergines and celery in a sweet and sour sauce with olives and capers.
Fritedda Artichokes, peas and broad beans cooked in a sweet and sour sauce.
Broccoli alla siciliana Broccoli cooked with cheese, black olives and wine.

Panelle di ceci Chick pea fritters.

Maccheroni alla paolina Macaroni with cabbage, pine nuts and raisins.

Spaghetti alla syracusana Spaghetti with a sauce of tomato, garlic, aubergines, peppers, olives and capers.

La scaccia Pasta baked in a pie shell with broccoli, tomato and cheese.

Riso quaresimale Rice cooked with fresh white beans, potato, onion, tomato and chilli pepper.

Millassata A *frittata* (omelette), with artichoke hearts, asparagus tips, parsley and grated cheese.

Crispedde Ricotta fritters – a speciality of Catania.

Cannoli Cylinders of pastry usually filled with Ricotta cheese, crystallized fruits, chopped nuts and liqueur.

Cassata (cake) A sponge cake filled with Ricotta cheese, flavoured with maraschino, crystallized fruit, chocolate and whipped cream.

Cassata (ice cream) A multi-coloured ice cream flavoured with liqueurs, crystallized fruit and grated chocolate.

SARDINIA

D.H. Lawrence wrote of Sardinia: 'So different from Sicily; none of the suave Greek Italian charms, none of the airs and graces, none of the glamour. Rather bare, rather stark, sometimes like Malta but without Malta's liveliness ... lost between Europe and Africa'.

Sardinia is the second largest island in the Mediterranean (Sicily is the largest). The landscape is mainly mountainous, barren, treeless and windswept. Sheep graze on the hills and plains. The population is sparse. The winters are mild and the summers are hot and parched.

Vegetables generally do not grow well, but aubergines, courgettes, white and purple cauliflowers, peas, fennel (often wild), broad and French beans are cultivated, and artichokes thrive. Fruits, including pomegranates, prickly pears, cherries, figs, melons and citrus fruits are plentiful, as are walnuts, almonds, hazelnuts, and chestnuts.

Bread is the staple food, especially *carasau* or *carta di musica* (music paper bread) – crisp, thin round sheets resembling tortillas. The Sardinians prefer bread to pasta, although they do make their own pasta, gnocchi and polenta.

Sardinians are very fond of cakes and pastries, especially made with almonds, honey and dried fruit.

Several cheeses are produced: the famous Pecorino Sardo (so beloved by the Ligurians), Fiore Sardo, Caciocavallo and Fetta, which is similar to the Greek Feta cheese.

The wines of Sardinia are inclined to be sweet and heavy. Vernaccia is the best-known wine and often drunk as an aperitif.

Vermentino di Gallura and Nasco are fine white dessert wines.

Local specialities

Zuppa di finochietti selvatici A cross between a soup and a casserole – layers of boiled fennel, toast and fresh Pecorino cheese in broth, and baked in the oven.

Zuppa sarda A broth, thickened with eggs, Mozzarella cheese, parsley and grated cheese, poured over toast.

La cauledda Cauliflower soup.

La favata Broad bean soup.

Culingiones Ravioli stuffed with spinach, fresh cheese, eggs and saffron, usually served with tomato sauce.

Maccarones a ferritus con aglio e olio Home-made noodles with tomato sauce, flavoured with garlic, olive oil and chilli pepper (*peperoncini*).

Culuriones Potato ravioli stuffed with onion, mint, egg and grated Pecorino cheese, served with tomato sauce.

Fagioli alla gallurese Dried white beans cooked with olive oil, garlic, tomato, fennel, onion and cabbage.

Cardi alla sarda Boiled cardoons topped with hard-boiled egg, parsley, olive oil, melted butter and breadcrumbs.

Torta di piselli A baked pea omelette.

Torta di faiscedda A sweet broad bean omelette.

Sospiri Almond meringues.

Aranzata di Nuoro Orange peel crystallized in honey and mixed with toasted almonds.

Pabassinos A diamond-shaped biscuit studded with raisins, almonds and walnuts. Pabassa is the dialect word for raisin.

Abufaus A kind of gingerbread made with honey, pine nuts, walnuts, currants and spices.

ANTIPASTI
AND SALADS
ANTIPASTI E INSALATE

'Salad refreshes without fatiguing and strengthens without irritating. I usually say it renews one's youth.'

Brillat-Savarin, *La Physiologie du Goût**

The Italians have created some of the most varied and imaginative antipasti or hors d'oeuvres in Europe. Fortunately, most of the dishes are very easy to prepare. Antipasti made in the home are generally very simple. A typical antipasto might consist of one or two marinated vegetables, some olives, or a small plate of tomato salad with a few slices of cheese or a stuffed egg on the side. Antipasto literally means 'before the meal', so always keep the quantities small. The purpose is to whet the appetite, not to satisfy it.

Most regions of Italy serve some form of pickled or marinated vegetables as an antipasto. Some are simply boiled in vinegar and spices and dressed with olive oil; some are marinated in wine and herbs; others are cooked in a sweet and sour sauce.

In northern Italy, especially in the Alpine regions, there are various forms of cheese dips and spreads that are served with toast or vegetables. In the south, where fewer dairy products are available, these cheese dishes are replaced by bean dips and spreads.

Crisp, raw salads or salads of cooked vegetables are often eaten before the meal. Most restaurants and *trattorie* in Rome serve cooked salads of dark green, leafy vegetables dressed with olive oil, lemon juice and garlic.

*Published in English as *The Philosopher in the Kitchen* (Penguin, 1970).

Further south, these cooked salads are often spiced with red chilli pepper (*peperoncini*).

Rice salads are often served at the beginning of the meal in northern Italy. The variations are infinite: artichoke hearts, asparagus, mushrooms, truffles, fennel, celery, pimientos, olives, capers, raisins and pine nuts all make excellent additions.

Virgin olive oil and a good quality wine vinegar (or lemon juice) are essential for making good antipasti and salads. Mustard or cream is rarely used in Italian dressings except in Piedmont and Lombardy, where the French culinary influence is still strong. Plain mayonnaise and flavoured mayonnaises are used throughout Italy.

Many dishes found elsewhere in this book, especially some of the stuffed vegetables and fritters, cheese *crostini* and some vegetable dishes, make excellent antipasti. The Italians make no distinction between a vegetable entrée or an antipasto – it is just the size of the dish that determines whether it is an antipasto, a main course or a side vegetable.

Lombardy   **MIXED VEGETABLES**   Serves 6
IN VINEGAR
Giardinetto di sott'aceto

Pickled vegetables or *sotti'aceti* are made all over Italy. Onions, carrots and French beans make a colourful combination. Other vegetables suitable for pickling are mushrooms, cauliflower, artichoke hearts, young cucumbers, fennel and beetroots. Try to use an imported wine vinegar as it is much milder than domestic wine vinegar.

225g (8oz) small white onions
225g (8oz) young tender carrots, diced
225g (8oz) French beans, cut into 2.5cm (1 inch) lengths
350ml (12fl oz) wine vinegar
350ml (12fl oz) water
3 tablespoons olive oil
2 bay leaves

6 whole cloves
1 tablespoon fresh basil leaves, or ¹/₂ teaspoon dried
6 black peppercorns

Combine all the ingredients in a saucepan. Bring to the boil, cover and simmer for 10 minutes or until the vegetables are just tender. Do not overcook – the vegetables should still be crisp. Remove the vegetables with a slotted spoon and set aside.

Increase the heat and reduce the liquid to about 450 ml (³/₄ pint). Place the vegetables in a bowl and pour over the reduced liquid. Make sure the liquid covers the vegetables. Refrigerate at least 12 hours before serving.

Liguria   **MARINATED MUSHROOMS**   Serves 6
Funghi marinati

450 g (1 lb) mushrooms, sliced
250 ml (8 fl oz) dry white wine
1 bay leaf
1 garlic clove, crushed
3 peppercorns
2.5 cm (1 inch) stick cinnamon
¹/₈ teaspoon freshly grated nutmeg
a pinch of rosemary
50 ml (2 fl oz) olive oil

Combine the mushrooms, wine, bay leaf, garlic and peppercorns in a saucepan. Bring to the boil and simmer for 5 minutes. Add the cinnamon stick, nutmeg and rosemary and simmer for a further 5 minutes.

Place in a serving bow, cover with olive oil and chill for at least 12 hours before serving.

Piedmont   **ARTICHOKES WITH**   Serves 4
EGG AND WINE SAUCE
Carciofi allo zabaglione

4 globe artichokes
4 egg yolks
1 teaspoon warm water
120 ml (4 fl oz) dry white wine
25 g (1 oz) butter, softened

Trim the stems of the artichokes and steam the vegetables for 45 minutes to 1 hour or until the bottoms are tender when pierced with a sharp knife and the outer leaves pull away easily. Set aside to cool.

Place the egg yolks and warm water in the top of a double saucepan over hot, not boiling water. Beat with a wire whisk until the mixture becomes foamy. Slowly pour in the white wine in a thin trickle, whisking constantly until the mixture forms soft mounds. Beat in the softened butter and pour into individual pots. Arrange the artichokes on individual plates and serve at once with a bowl of sauce on the side.

Trentino,   **ASPARAGUS WITH**   Serves 4
Alto   **HARD-BOILED EGG SAUCE**
Adige   *Asparagi alla salsa bolzanina*

This recipe is from Bolzano in the Alto Adige. Sometimes capers are added to give a more piquant sauce.

900g (2lbs) asparagus
2 hard-boiled eggs
2 egg yolks
1 teaspoon Dijon mustard
2 tablespoons lemon juice
225g (8 fl oz) sunflower or safflower seed oil
1 tablespoon fresh chives, chopped
1 teaspoon fresh tarragon, chopped
salt
freshly ground black pepper

Trim the ends of the asparagus and with a sharp knife remove any fibrous inedible parts from the lower stalks. Steam for 15 to 20 minutes or until tender.

Meanwhile separate the yolks from the whites of the hard-boiled eggs, and place them in a mixing bowl with the raw egg yolks, the mustard, and a few drops of lemon juice. Mix well together. Very slowly beat in the oil, drop by drop, with a wire whisk. When the mixture becomes very thick, thin it with a few drops of lemon juice. When the oil is used up, stir in the finely chopped hard-boiled egg whites and the herbs. Season to taste with salt and black pepper. Arrange the asparagus on individual plates and serve with the sauce on the side.

Veneto   **VENETIAN PEPERONATA**   Serves 6
Peperonata alla veneta

The Venetian version of this famous Florentine dish includes aubergine and uses dry white wine instead of wine vinegar. Olives and capers sometimes are included.

6 green or yellow peppers
1 small aubergine (about 100g (4oz))
65ml (2½fl oz) olive oil
1 garlic clove, crushed
1 large onion, thinly sliced
225g (8oz) canned plum tomatoes, seeded and chopped
3 tablespoons dry white wine
salt
freshly ground black pepper

Remove the pith and seeds from the peppers and cut into strips. Cut the aubergine into 1 cm ($\frac{1}{2}$ inch) cubes. Do not peel.

Heat the olive oil in a large frying pan and cook the garlic and onion over a moderate heat for 3 minutes. Add the aubergine and peppers and continue to cook, covered, for 15 minutes, or until the aubergine and peppers are just tender. Stir occasionally so the vegetables cook evenly. Add the tomatoes, cover and simmer for 20 minutes or until the sauce is thickened. Pour in the wine, increase the heat slightly and cook for a further 5 minutes. Season with salt and black pepper to taste. The peperonata should be fairly dry at the end of cooking. This may be served hot or cold.

Sicily   **LA CAPONATA,**   Serves 4 to 6
                  CATANIA STYLE
La caponata catanese

La caponata, or *caponatina*, is Sicily's most famous antipasto. Its ingredients vary around the island. Artichokes, potatoes and hard-boiled eggs are all possible additions. Raisins and pine nuts are optional. In Syracuse it is made with grated chocolate instead of tomato sauce. In Catania, peppers are added.

1 large aubergine (about 450 g (1 lb))
150 ml ($\frac{1}{4}$ pint) olive oil
1 small onion, chopped
1 stalk celery, thinly sliced
1 red pepper, cut into small dice
175 g (6 oz) canned plum tomatoes, forced through a sieve or
    puréed in a blender
2 tablespoons sultanas
2 tablespoons pine nuts
50 g (2 oz) Italian or Greek green olives, stoned and sliced
2 tablespoons capers
3 tablespoons wine vinegar
1 tablespoon sugar
salt
freshly ground black pepper

Wash the aubergine but do not peel. Cut it into 1 cm (½ inch) cubes. Heat 120 ml (4 fl oz) of the olive oil in a large frying pan and cook the aubergine over a moderate heat until it is soft and starting to turn golden. Remove from the pan. Add the remaining olive oil and cook the onion, celery and pepper for 5 minutes or until the vegetables are soft. Add the puréed tomatoes and cook over a moderate heat for 8 to 10 minutes or until the sauce starts to thicken. Stir in the cooked aubergine, sultanas, pine nuts, olives, capers, vinegar and sugar. Season with salt and black pepper to taste. Simmer for 5 minutes to blend the flavours.

Transfer to a serving dish and serve at room temperature.

Liguria   **EGGS, STUFFED**   Serves 6
                    WITH PESTO
                 Uove ripiene col pesto

6 hard-boiled eggs
50 ml (2 fl oz) pesto sauce (see page 58)
50 ml (2 fl oz) mayonnaise
salt
freshly ground black pepper
1 tablespoon capers

Cut the eggs in half lengthwise. Remove the yolks and mash them in a bowl. Blend in the pesto sauce, mayonnaise and salt and black pepper to taste. Spoon the mixture back into the egg halves and garnish with capers.

Friuli and   **LIPTAUER CHEESE,**   Serves 8
Venezia Giulia   **FRIULI STYLE**   to 10
                 Liptauer friuliana

This recipe dates back to the turn of the century when Friuli was part of the Austro-Hungarian Empire. If you prefer, the kümmel can be replaced by single cream.

40g (1½oz) butter, softened
100g (4oz) Ricotta cheese
100g (4oz) Mascarpone cheese
1 or 2 tablespoons kümmel or brandy
2 tablespoons finely chopped onion
1 teaspoon Dijon mustard
1 teaspoon paprika
a pinch of ground cumin
salt
6 slices of rye bread, toasted

Beat the butter in a mixing bowl until it is soft and light. Gradually add the Ricotta and Mascarpone cheese and mix together until very smooth. Thin with enough kümmel to give a spreading consistency – the mixture should not be too soft or soupy. Add the remaining ingredients and blend well.

Form into a mound on a serving dish. Sprinkle with a little additional paprika and serve with slices of rye toast.

Lombardy   **GORGONZOLA TOASTS**   Serves 6
Crostini di gorgonzola

Perfect with a bottle of dry red wine.

100g (4oz) Gorgonzola cheese
100g (4oz) butter, softened
2 tablespoons brandy
6 slices of wholemeal bread, toasted

Crumble the Gorgonzola cheese into a mixing bowl. Add the softened butter and mix well, then blend in the brandy.

Cut the toast into quarters diagonally and spread with the Gorgonzola cheese mixture.

Apulia	**LA CAPRIATA**	Serves 4

La capriata

La capriata is a simple broad bean purée. It is usually served with a salad of cooked turnip tops dressed with plenty of garlic and virgin olive oil. It is also found in Basilicata and parts of Calabria. The dish dates back to the days when most of southern Italy was under Greek rule. Use shelled dried broad beans, which are available in Italian groceries and delicatessen.

175 g (6 oz) dried broad beans
750 ml (1 ¼ pints) water
1 small onion, sliced
4 tablespoons virgin olive oil
salt
cayenne pepper
4 slices of wholemeal bread, toasted

Soak the broad beans in water overnight and drain. Bring to boil in the water and add the onion. Cover and simmer for 1 to 1½ hours, or until the beans are very tender, and most of the liquid has evaporated.

Force the beans and onion through a sieve or purée in a blender. Add half the olive oil and season with salt to taste. The consistency should be very creamy.

Transfer to a serving bowl. Pour over the remaining olive oil and sprinkle lightly with cayenne pepper. Serve at room temperature with slices of toast on the side.

OLIVES AND OLIVE OIL
Olive e olio d'oliva

Olive trees have long been a symbol of wealth in the Mediterranean. They have been cultivated in Italy since Roman times, when bread and olives were a staple food of the peasants.

An olive tree has a life span of 300 to 700 years, although some olive trees have been said to live a thousand years. They thrive on well-drained soil in full sun and can survive for more than six months without water.

The unripe green olives are picked in the autumn, soaked in a lye solution to remove their bitterness, and then pickled in brine. If left on the tree, they ripen and turn jet black by December and are then picked for marinating or crushing into oil.

The best-quality olive oil is virgin olive oil which is cold-pressed from the first pressing. It is a rich green colour and has a strong fruity favour. It is probably the most healthy of all vegetable oils as olives can be pressed easily without using heat or chemicals. It has the additional benefit of having no cholesterol. Peasants in southern Italy who consume vast quantities of olive oil (up to one-fifth of their daily diet) have been found to have very low levels of blood cholesterol. It is also an ideal cooking oil as it can safely be heated to higher temperatures than most other oils.

Olive oil keeps best in a cool dry place. It should not be kept in the refrigerator as it will coagulate.

Lazio **CELERY IN PINZIMONIO** Serves 4
Sedani in pinzimonio to 6

Romans love to eat raw vegetables dipped in virgin olive oil. It is the perfect start to a meal; nothing could be better for your health or your digestion. Try this recipe with radishes, fennel, pimiento, cucumber or carrot sticks.

1 bunch celery
250 ml (8 fl oz) virgin olive oil
1 clove garlic, crushed
salt
a pinch of hot red pepper flakes

Trim and wash the celery. Cut it into 10 cm (4 inch) lengths and arrange in a serving dish. Pour the olive oil into a small serving bowl and mix with the garlic and salt and hot red pepper flakes to taste. Serve as a dip.

Valle d'Aosta   **RADISH AND**   Serves 3 to 4
                 GRUYERE SALAD
Insalata di ravanelli e groviera

225g (8oz) radishes, sliced
50g (2oz) Gruyère cheese, cut into small dice
50g (2oz) Italian or Greek black olives, stoned and sliced
120ml (4fl oz) vinaigrette sauce (see page 60)

Combine the radishes, Gruyère cheese and black olives in a salad bowl. Pour over the vinaigrette sauce and toss well.

Lazio   **ROMAN MIXED**   Serves 4 to 6
                 GREEN SALAD
Insalata di misticanza

In Rome, *insalata di misticanza* consists of at least 15 different salad greens and herbs, usually including rocket, sorrel, lamb's lettuce, purslane, curly endive, chicory, dandelion, mint, basil and valerian. *Misticanza* is the Roman name for rocket.

100g (4oz) rocket
100g (4oz) lamb's lettuce
100g (4oz) red chicory
100g (4oz) fresh spinach
½ bunch of watercress
¼ curly endive
1 small fennel bulb, diced
2 spring onions, thinly sliced
a handful of fresh parsley, chopped
a handful of fresh mint, chopped
2 tablespoons fresh basil, chopped
2 tablespoons fresh chives, chopped
65ml (2½fl oz) vinaigrette sauce (see page 60)

Break the rocket, lamb's lettuce, red chicory, spinach, watercress and endive into bite-size pieces. Place in a salad bowl with the fennel, spring onions, parsley, mint, basil and chives. Pour over the vinaigrette sauce, toss lightly and serve at once.

Veneto **RED ENDIVE SALAD** Serves 4
Insalata di radicchio rosso

Red endive or *radicchio rosso* is the most highly prized salad 'greens' in Italy. It is mainly grown in the region around Treviso and is only available in the winter months. It has beautiful reddish-purple leaves, marbled with white, and a unique, slightly bitter taste. In recent years new varieties have been grown in Italy and abroad that are available all year round.

225g (8oz) radicchio (red) endive
100g (4oz) rocket
½ leek, thinly sliced
1 purple onion, thinly sliced
8 radishes, sliced
12 Italian or Greek black olives
65ml (2½fl oz) vinaigrette sauce (see page 60)

Break the radicchio and rocket into bite-size pieces. Place in a salad bowl with the leek, onion, radishes and black olives. Pour over the vinaigrette sauce and serve at once.

Lazio   **SWISS CHARD SALAD**   Serves 4
         Insalata di bietole   to 6

The Romans love salads of cooked green vegetables dressed with olive oil, lemon juice and garlic. French beans, spring greens, beet leaves and spinach are all served the same way. Always dress the vegetables while they are still warm.

2 large bunches Swiss chard
3 tablespoons olive oil
1 tablespoon lemon juice
2 garlic cloves, crushed
salt
freshly ground black pepper

Wash the Swiss chard and remove the thick stems. Steam for 6 to 8 minutes in a covered saucepan or until tender. Drain well and allow to cool slightly.

Place in a salad bowl and dress with the olive oil, lemon juice and garlic. Season to taste with salt and black pepper. Toss lightly and serve.

Liguria   **MIXED SALAD**   Serves 6
           LIGURIAN STYLE
           Condijon

6 large tomatoes, peeled and sliced
6 spring onions, thinly sliced
1 yellow or green pepper, cut into thin strips
½ cucumber, peeled and thinly sliced
8 radishes, sliced
12 black olives
1 teaspoon capers
2 hard-boiled eggs, quartered
65 ml (2½ fl oz) vinaigrette sauce (see page 60)

Combine all the vegetables in a salad bowl. Add the olives, capers, hard-boiled eggs and the vinaigrette sauce. Toss well and serve at once.

Lombardy **LETTUCE AND** Serves 4 to 6
GORGONZOLA SALAD
Insalata di lattugha e gorgonzola

This simple salad of lettuce and chopped walnuts is tossed
with a delicious dressing of Gorgonzola cheese, vinaigrette
sauce, cream and tarragon.

1 lettuce
25g (1oz) shelled walnuts, coarsely chopped
50g (2oz) Gorgonzola cheese
65ml (2½fl oz) vinaigrette sauce (see page 60)
3 tablespoons single cream
1 teaspoon fresh tarragon leaves, or ½ teaspoon dried

Break the lettuce into bite-size pieces and place in a salad
bowl with the chopped walnuts.

Mash the Gorgonzola cheese with a fork in a bowl.
Gradually blend in the vinaigrette sauce, cream and
tarragon until the sauce is smooth and creamy. Pour over
the lettuce and walnuts, toss lightly, and serve at once.

Piedmont **MUSHROOM, CELERY AND** Serves 4
PARMESAN CHEESE SALAD
WITH BRANDY CREAM DRESSING
Insalata di funghi alla torinese

A speciality of Turin.

2 tablespoons olive oil
450g (1lb) button mushrooms, sliced
1 tablespoon water
4 stalks celery, thinly sliced
50g (2oz) Parmesan cheese, cut into slithers
2 tablespoons green olives, stoned and sliced
*150ml (¼ pint) vinaigrette sauce (see page 60) made with
    lemon juice*
2 tablespoons single cream
1 teaspoon brandy

salt
freshly ground black pepper
1 truffle, sliced paper-thin

Heat the olive oil in a large frying pan. Add the mushrooms and water and cook over a moderate heat for 5
minutes. Drain away any excess liquid and allow the
mushrooms to cool.

Combine the celery, mushrooms, Parmesan cheese and
olives in a salad bowl. Mix the vinaigrette sauce with the
cream and brandy. Season to taste with salt and black
pepper. Pour over the salad and toss lightly. Garnish with
the truffle and serve at once.

Piedmont **PEPPER AND FONTINA** Serves 6
CHEESE SALAD
Insalata di fontina

This traditional Piedmontese salad is served in the late
summer and autumn when peppers are ripe and plentiful.
They are combined with Fontina cheese and green olives
and mixed with a deliciously light mustard and cream
dressing.

6 yellow or red peppers
175g (6oz) Fontina cheese, cut into small dice
10 green olives, pitted and sliced
1 teaspoon Dijon mustard
2 tablespoons single cream
65ml (2½fl oz) olive oil
1 teaspoon lemon juice
salt
freshly ground black pepper
1 teaspoon fresh tarragon leaves, or ½ teaspoon dried

Cook the peppers under the grill until the skins are blackened all over. Wash off the skins under cold water, pat dry
and cut into thin strips. Place in a salad bowl with the
Fontina cheese and green olives.

Mix the mustard and cream together in a bowl. Blend in the olive oil, lemon juice and tarragon and add salt and black pepper to taste. Pour over the pepper mixture, toss well and serve at once.

Lazio   **MOZZARELLA WITH**   Serves 4
**TOMATOES AND
BLACK OLIVES**
Mozzarella con pomodori e olive neri

This simple lunch dish is served on the beach at Fregene, outside Rome.

350g (12oz) fresh Mozzarella cheese
4 large tomatoes
50ml (2fl oz) olive oil
1 tablespoon fresh basil, or ½ teaspoon dried
20 black olives
salt
freshly ground black pepper

Cut the Mozzarella and tomatoes into slices 5mm (¼ inch) thick. Arrange the Mozzarella on individual plates and top with slices of tomato. Pour a little olive oil over the top and sprinkle with fresh basil. Garnish with black olives and season to taste with salt and black pepper.

Sicily **STUFFED TOMATOES** Serves 6
WITH VEGETABLES
AND MAYONNAISE
Insalata siciliana

6 large ripe tomatoes
175g (6oz) marinated mushrooms (see page 36)
1 cucumber, cut into small dice
3 stalks celery, diced
175g (6oz) cooked green beans, cut into 1cm (½ inch)
lengths
1 tablespoon capers
120ml (4fl oz) homemade mayonnaise (see page 60)
18 black olives

Slice off the top quarter of the tomatoes. Reserve the tops for lids. Combine the mushrooms, cucumber, celery, beans and capers in a bowl. Spoon the mayonnaise over the mixed vegetables and toss lightly.

Spoon some of the mixture into each tomato and replace the reserved lids. Arrange on a serving platter and surround with the remaining mixed vegetables. Garnish with black olives and serve.

Campania   **BROAD BEAN SALAD**   Serves 3 to 4
Insalata di fave

A speciality of Naples.

350g (12oz) shelled broad beans
1 teaspoon fresh mint leaves, chopped or ¼ teaspoon dried
120ml (4fl oz) vinaigrette sauce (see page 60)

Bring the broad beans to the boil in lightly salted water and cook, covered, for 25–30 minutes or until they are tender. Drain and place in a serving bowl.

Mix the fresh mint with the vinaigrette sauce and pour over the beans while they are still hot. Toss lightly and serve warm or at room temperature.

Sicily   **COUNTRY BEAN AND**   Serves 6
POTATO SALAD
Insalata alla contadina

This hearty salad is perfect for a buffet.

450g (1lb) new potatoes, boiled and diced
450g (1lb) French beans, steamed and cut into 2.5cm (1 inch) lengths
250g (9oz) cooked dried haricot beans
1 small onion, finely chopped
50g (2oz) Italian or Greek black olives, stoned and sliced
1 tablespoon capers
250ml (8fl oz) vinaigrette sauce (see page 60)
2 tablespoons fresh parsley, finely chopped

Combine the potatoes, French beans, cooked haricot beans, onion, black olives and capers in a salad bowl. Pour over the vinaigrette sauce and toss well. Sprinkle with parsley. Serve at room temperature.

Sicily   **POTATO SALAD**   Serves 6
                     WITH MARSALA
                     Insalata di patate

900g (2lb) waxy potatoes, boiled and sliced
2 tablespoons dry Marsala
1 onion, chopped
2 stalks celery, thinly sliced
2 teaspoons fresh basil, chopped
2 tablespoons fresh parsley, finely chopped
150ml (¼ pint) vinaigrette sauce (see page 60)

Place the potatoes in a salad bowl and sprinkle with the
Marsala while they are still warm. Add the onion, celery,
basil, parsley and vinaigrette sauce. Toss lightly and serve.

Piedmont   **PIEDMONTESE RICE**   Serves 6
                        SALAD
                Insalata di riso alla piemontese

There are many versions of rice salad in northern Italy.
Raisins, capers, sliced gherkins, artichoke hearts,
radishes, fennel and tomatoes all make excellent additions.

300g (10oz) long grain rice, cooked
100g (4oz) asparagus tips, cooked
3 stalks celery, thinly sliced
2 spring onions, thinly sliced
1 red pepper, diced
50ml (2fl oz) homemade mayonnaise (see page 60)
1 teaspoon Dijon mustard
1 teaspoon fresh marjoram, or ¼ teaspoon dried
1 teaspoon dry Marsala
2 tablespoons green olives, stoned and sliced
1 truffle, sliced paper-thin (optional)

Combine the rice, asparagus, celery, onions and pepper in
a salad bowl. Mix the mayonnaise with the mustard,
marjoram and Marsala and pour over the salad. Toss
lightly and garnish with the green olives and truffle, if
liked. Chill for 1 to 2 hours before serving.

SAUCES

SALSE

Italian food is not clothed in sauces like French cooking. A few simple sauces are used to enhance the natural flavour of the food.

Tomato sauce has become synonymous with Italian cooking. In fact, tomato sauce is rarely used in northern Italian cooking. Tomato sauce does, however, predominate in the cooking of the south, but the flavouring varies from region to region. In many areas of the south, especially Apulia and Basilicata, *peperoncini* (a hot pungent chilli pepper) is added to tomato sauce. In Sicily, olives, capers, raisins and pine nuts may be added, producing a strong, sweet and sour flavour. In Liguria, fresh or dried mushrooms are often added to tomato sauce to make the local sauce called *tocco di funghi*.

Liguria is more famous for its green sauces, the basil sauce *pesto*, and *salsa di noci* – a parsley and walnut sauce.

Emilia-Romagna claims to have invented the classic white béchamel or *balsamella* sauce as far back as the fourteenth century (this is still disputed by the French, who claim it was invented by Louis XIV's chef). Béchamel sauce is a basic ingredient of many dishes all over Italy, especially *lasagne, timbali, sformati* and many gratins.

Fundamental to Italian cooking, but not strictly a sauce, is the *soffrito* or *battuto*. This is a finely chopped combination of garlic, onion, celery, carrot and herbs that is quickly sautéed in olive oil or olive oil and butter. The *soffrito* is the foundation of many Italian soups and stews.

Campania   **TOMATO SAUCE**
La pommarola
Makes enough for 450g (1lb) of pasta

This is my favourite tomato sauce. It is very light, still tastes of tomatoes, and takes less than 15 minutes to prepare.

2 tablespoons olive oil
1 garlic clove, crushed
1 tablespoon fresh basil or ½ teaspoon dried
2 tablespoons fresh parsley, finely chopped
675g (1½lb) canned plum tomatoes, seeded and chopped
salt
freshly ground black pepper

Heat the olive oil in a large frying pan and cook the garlic, basil and parsley for 1 minute. Add the chopped tomatoes and season with salt and black pepper to taste. Cook, uncovered, over a high heat for 8 to 10 minutes or until the sauce starts to thicken, mashing the tomatoes gently with a fork as they cook.

Campania
and the
South
TOMATO SAUCE WITH OLIVES AND CAPERS
La pizzaiola
Makes enough for 450g (1lb) pasta

Hot and piquant.

3 tablespoons olive oil
2 garlic cloves, crushed
a pinch of hot red pepper flakes
1 teaspoon fresh oregano, or ¼ teaspoon dried
675g (1½lb) canned plum tomatoes, seeded and chopped
50g (2oz) Italian or Greek black olives, stoned and roughly chopped
2 teaspoons capers
salt

Heat the olive oil in a large frying pan. Add the garlic, red pepper flakes and oregano and cook for 1 minute. Add the chopped tomatoes, olives and capers and season with salt to taste. Cook, uncovered, over a high heat for 8 to 10 minutes or until the sauce starts to thicken, mashing the tomatoes gently with a fork as they cook.

Lazio
TOMATO SAUCE WITH WINE
Sugo finto
Makes enough sauce for 450g (1lb) of pasta

This tomato sauce is cooked more slowly and is richly flavoured with vegetables and wine.

50ml (2fl oz) olive oil
1 garlic clove, crushed
1 tablespoon fresh parsley, finely chopped
1 teaspoon fresh oregano, or ¼ teaspoon dried
1 medium onion, finely chopped
1 stalk celery, finely sliced
1 small carrot, finely chopped
1 whole clove
65ml 2½fl oz) dry white wine

675g (1½lb) canned plum tomatoes, seeded and chopped
salt
freshly ground black pepper

Heat the olive oil in a large frying pan and cook the garlic, parsley and oregano for 1 minute. Add the onion, celery, carrot and clove and cook gently for 8 to 10 minutes or until the vegetables start to soften.

Add the wine and cook over a high heat until it has almost evaporated. Add the tomatoes, salt and black pepper to taste and continue cooking over a moderate heat for 20 to 30 minutes or until the sauce has thickened. Remove the clove and force through a sieve or purée in a food processor. Return to the pan and heat through.

Liguria   **MUSHROOM AND**
TOMATO SAUCE
Tocco di funghi freschi
Makes enough sauce for 450g (1lb) of pasta

50ml (2fl oz) olive oil
4 garlic cloves, crushed
a handful of fresh parsley, finely chopped
1 teaspoon fresh marjoram or ¼ teaspoon dried
450g (1lb) fresh mushrooms, thinly sliced
450g (1lb) canned plum tomatoes, seeded and chopped
salt
freshly ground black pepper

Heat the olive oil in a large frying pan and cook the garlic, parsley and marjoram for 1 minute. Add the sliced mushrooms and cook over a moderate heat for 5 minutes or until they are tender.

Add the tomatoes, salt and black pepper to taste and cook over a high heat for 8 to 10 minutes or until the sauce starts to thicken, mashing the tomatoes gently with a fork as they cook.

Emilia- **BÉCHAMEL SAUCE**
Romagna *La balsamella*
Makes about 450ml (¾ pint)

This recipe makes a medium thick béchamel sauce that is especially good for lasagne. For a thinner sauce simply add more milk until you get the desired consistency.

50g (2oz) butter
40g (1½oz) flour
450ml (¾ pint) hot milk
½ teaspoon salt
pinch of white pepper
¼ teaspoon freshly grated nutmeg

Melt the butter in a heavy based pan. Stir in the flour and cook for 1 minute without browning. Pour in a little hot milk and stir vigorously with a wooden spoon over a moderate heat, until the mixture is thick and free of lumps. Gradually add more milk until all the milk is incorporated and the sauce is very smooth and creamy. Season with salt, pepper and nutmeg and simmer for 1 or 2 more minutes.

PINE NUTS
Pignoli

Pine nuts or *pignoli* come from the stone pine (*Pinus pinea*), a native Italian tree. They are a soft cream-coloured nut, not unlike the almond in flavour. They are frequently used in Italian cooking in stuffings, rice dishes, sauces and confectionery, and are also one of the basic ingredients of the famous Ligurian sauce, *pesto alla genovese*. They are a very good additional source of protein for vegetarians.

Liguria   **BASIL SAUCE**
Pesto alla genovese
Makes enough for 675g to 900g (1½ to 2lb) of pasta.

This famous Ligurian sauce is traditionally made with a mortar and pestle, but a blender makes a perfect sauce in a fraction of the time. Only fresh basil can be used to make this sauce. Pesto is used as a sauce for pasta, gnocchi, to enrich vegetable soups, and with stuffed eggs.

125g (4oz) fresh basil leaves
a handful of fresh parsley
1 teaspoon fresh marjoram, or ¼ teaspoon dried
2 garlic cloves, crushed
65ml (2½fl oz) olive oil
3 tablespoons pine nuts
2 to 3 tablespoons hot water
40g (1½oz) freshly grated Pecorino Sardo or Parmesan cheese

Place the basil, parsley, marjoram, garlic, olive oil and pine nuts in a blender and mix in slowly until the ingredients are chopped. Add 2 to 3 tablespoons hot water and the grated cheese. Blend at high speed until the mixture is smooth.

Liguria   **SPINACH PESTO**
Pesto con spinaci
Makes enough for 675g to 900g (1½ to 2lb) of pasta

Spinach makes a delicious *pesto* when fresh basil is unavailable.

125g (4oz) fresh spinach
15g (½oz) fresh parsley
2 tablespoons pine nuts
10 walnut halves
2 garlic cloves, crushed
65ml (2½fl oz) olive oil
2 to 3 tablespoons hot water

50g (2oz) freshly grated Pecorino Sardo or Parmesan
   cheese
salt
freshly ground black pepper
¼ teaspoon freshly grated nutmeg

Place the spinach, parsley, pine nuts, walnuts, garlic and
olive oil in a blender and mix slowly until the ingredients
are chopped. Add 2 or 3 tablespoons of hot water and the
grated cheese. Blend at high speed until the mixture is
smooth. Season with nutmeg and salt and black pepper to
taste.

Piedmont   **BAGNET**
Bagnet
Makes about 225ml (8fl oz)

Bagnet is a parsley and garlic sauce, not unlike the
Ligurian *pesto*. It is indispensable to the Piedmontese
household, where it is used more as a condiment than a
sauce. Add a teaspoon or two to sauces, soups, vegetable
stews or even salad dressings. Or use it sparingly as a
sauce for pasta or stirred into a risotto. Bagnet keeps well
for up to a week in an airtight jar in the refrigerator.

125g (4oz) fresh parsley, roughly chopped
8 to 10 garlic cloves, crushed
about 65ml (2½fl oz) olive oil
salt
freshly ground black pepper

Place the parsley, garlic, olive oil, salt and pepper in a
blender and mix slowly until the ingredients are chopped.
Blend at high speed until the mixture is smooth. Spoon
into an airtight glass jar and pour a thin layer of olive oil
over the top.

All Italy   **VINAIGRETTE SAUCE**
                 Salsa vinaigrette
                 Makes about 300 ml (½ pint)

A good vinaigrette sauce depends on the quality of the oil and vinegar used. Choose a fruity extra virgin olive oil and a mild wine vinegar. An excellent wine vinegar, *aceto balsamico di Modena*, is becoming more readily available at Italian speciality stores and delicatessens. This is a herb-flavoured wine vinegar that has been made in Modena since the eleventh century. One bottle takes a minimum of 10 years to produce. The result is a remarkably smooth and delicious vinegar that the people of Modena claim is rich in medicinal qualities.

65 ml (2½ fl oz) wine vinegar
250 ml (8 fl oz) extra virgin olive oil
2 garlic cloves, crushed
a few leaves fresh basil
salt
freshly ground black pepper

Combine all the ingredients, with seasoning to taste, in a small glass jar. Screw the cap on firmly and shake well until the ingredients have blended and the vinaigrette sauce is slightly thickened.

All Italy   **MAYONNAISE**
                 Maionese
                 Makes about 350 ml (12 fl oz)

To make a good mayonnaise both the egg yolks and the oil should be at room temperature. Beat the oil in very slowly at the beginning – this will help to prevent the yolks from separating. Should this happen, simply start again with a fresh egg yolk and beat in the 'separated' mixture, drop by drop, before adding the remaining oil.

2 egg yolks
about 2 tablespoons lemon juice (or to taste)

salt
a pinch of cayenne pepper
350 ml (12 fl oz) olive oil
1 tablespoon boiling water

Place the egg yolks in a mixing bowl with a few drops of lemon juice. Add salt and cayenne pepper to taste. Very slowly beat in the oil, drop by drop, with a wire whisk. Beat constantly. When the mixture becomes very thick, thin it with a few drops of lemon juice. Once the oil is used up, gradually beat in the boiling water. This will improve the consistency and help to prevent the mayonnaise from separating.

Liguria and the North **GREEN MAYONNAISE WITH PISTACHIO NUTS**
Maionese verde
Makes about 350 ml (12 fl oz)

250 ml (8 fl oz) homemade mayonnaise (see page 60)
a handful of fresh parsley, chopped
3 to 4 leaves fresh spinach, shredded
1 teaspoon fresh mint
2 teaspoons pistachio nuts, finely chopped

Place the mayonnaise, parsley, spinach, mint and pistachio nuts in a blender and blend on high speed until very smooth.

SOUPS
MINESTRE

Italian soups fall into three categories: broths or clear soups; cream soups; and vegetable soups. Broths are usually served with some kind of pasta which can vary from the tiny *acine di pepe* (peppercorns) to any of the large, stuffed ravioli.

Cream soups are usually puréed and thickened with eggs, cream or béchamel sauce; sometimes they are served with the addition of pasta or croûtons.

Vegetable soups also fall into three categories: *zuppa*, which always includes bread, toast or croûtons; *minestra*, a vegetable soup with rice or pasta; and *minestrone*, a big or more substantial version of *minestra*. *Minestroni* are often sufficiently substantial for a meal. Both *minestre* and *minestroni* are always served with grated cheese on the side.

All Italy   **VEGETABLE STOCK**
Brodo
Makes about 1.85 litres (3¼ pints) stock

Stock (or broth) plays an integral part in Italian cooking, as it is the foundation of many soups and rice dishes.

2.25 litres (4 pints) water
2 small potatoes
1 leek, thinly sliced
1 onion, chopped
1 small bunch celery, diced
4 carrots, sliced
2 bay leaves
a handful of fresh parsley, chopped
⅛ teaspoon dried thyme
1 teaspoon salt
6 peppercorns

Combine all the ingredients in a large saucepan and bring slowly to the boil. Simmer for 1½ to 2 hours. Strain through a fine sieve. The broth will keep for 2 or 3 days in the refrigerator.

Calabria   **POTATO AND**   Serves 6
ONION SOUP
Licurdia

This is a simple potato soup, flavoured with onions and hot pepper. A speciality of Cosenza.

450g (1 lb) potatoes, diced
450g (1 lb) onions, sliced
¼ Webb's lettuce, shredded
2 litres (3½ pints) water
3 tablespoons olive oil
⅛ teaspoon hot red pepper flakes
salt
6 slices of wholemeal bread, cut into small squares
100g (4oz) freshly grated Pecorino cheese

Place the potatoes, onions and lettuce in a saucepan with the water. Bring the liquid slowly to the boil, reduce the heat to very low and simmer for 45 minutes.

Add the olive oil, hot pepper and salt to taste. Simmer for 5 more minutes. Place the bread on a baking tray in a moderately hot oven at 190°C (275°F/Gas Mark 6) until crisp and dry. Place these croûtons in individual soup bowls, pour over the soup and serve at once, with the grated cheese on the side.

Veneto   **CREAM OF**   Serves 4
                          CELERY SOUP   to 6
                          Crema di sedani

This is a speciality of Verona.

25 g (1 oz) butter
450 g (1 lb) celery, diced
1 large leek, thinly sliced
1 medium potato, diced
1.2 litres (2 pints) vegetable stock or water
1 egg yolk
120 ml (4 fl oz) single cream
25 g (1 oz) freshly grated Parmesan cheese
1/4 teaspoon freshly grated nutmeg
salt
freshly ground black pepper

Heat the butter in a large saucepan and cook the celery, leek and potato over a moderate heat for 3 minutes. Add the stock and bring to the boil. Cover and simmer for 30 minutes. Force through a sieve or purée in a blender and return to the saucepan.

Beat the egg yolk, cream and grated cheese together. Beat 120 ml (4 fl oz) of hot soup into the egg and cream mixture, then stir the mixture back into the soup. Add the nutmeg; season with salt and black pepper to taste. Heat to just below simmering point. Do not boil or the soup will curdle. Serve at once.

Piedmont   **CREAM OF**   Serves 4
                  MUSHROOM SOUP
                   Crema di funghi

2 tablespoons olive oil
450g (1 lb) fresh mushrooms, sliced
50 ml (2 fl oz) dry Marsala
900 ml (1½ pints) béchamel sauce (see page 57)
250 ml (8 fl oz) hot vegetable stock (see page 63)
120 ml (4 fl oz) single cream, heated
salt
freshly ground black pepper
2 tablespoons fresh parsley, finely chopped

Heat the olive oil in a saucepan and cook the mushrooms over a moderate heat for 5 minutes. Add the Marsala, increase the heat and cook until it has almost evaporated.

Add the béchamel sauce and stock and simmer for 15 minutes. Force through a sieve or purée in a blender. Return to the saucepan and stir in the hot cream. Season with salt and black pepper to taste. Heat thoroughly. Sprinkle with parsley and serve at once.

Lombardy   **CREAM OF**   Serves 4
                  ASPARAGUS SOUP
                   Crema di asparagi

450g (1 lb) asparagus
1 leek, thinly sliced
2 tablespoons butter
225g (8 oz) potatoes, diced
900ml (1½ pints) water
4 tablespoons single cream
salt
freshly ground black pepper

Trim the ends of the asparagus and with a sharp knife remove any fibrous parts from the lower stalks. Cut into 2 inch lengths. Heat the butter in a large saucepan and cook the asparagus and leek over a moderate heat for 2 minutes. Add the potatoes and 1½ pints of water. Bring to a boil, cover, and simmer for 30 minutes, or until the vegetables are tender. Force through a sieve or purée in a blender. Return to the saucepan and stir in the cream. Season with salt and black pepper to taste. Heat thoroughly and serve at once.

Emilia-
Romagna
SWISS CHARD SOUP
Zuppa di bietole
Serves 6

1 large bunch Swiss chard
1.2 litres (2 pints) vegetable stock or water
1 egg yolk
120 ml (4 fl oz) single cream
50 g (2 oz) freshly grated Parmesan cheese
¼ teaspoon freshly grated nutmeg
salt
freshly ground black pepper
6 slices of wholemeal bread, cut into small squares

Wash the Swiss chard carefully and cook in a covered saucepan over a moderate heat for 5 minutes. The water clinging to the leaves will be sufficient to prevent scorching. Drain and chop very finely. Bring the stock to the boil, add the Swiss chard and simmer for 5 minutes.

Beat the egg yolk with the cream and grated cheese. Remove the soup from the heat. Beat 120 ml (4 fl oz) of hot soup into the egg yolk and cream mixture, then stir it back into the soup. Add the nutmeg; season with salt and pepper to taste. Heat gently to just below simmering point. Do not boil or the soup will curdle.

Dry the squares of bread in a moderately hot oven at 190°C (375°F/Gas Mark 5) to make croûtons. Serve the soup at once with the croûtons.

Lombardy
PUMPKIN SOUP
Minestra di zucca
Serves 6

This is a delicious velvety smooth soup, with a hint of spice. It may be made with marrow when pumpkin is out of season.

2 tablespoons olive oil
1 small pumpkin (about 675–900g (1½–2g), peeled, seeded
  and diced
3 potatoes, diced
1 bay leaf
1 tablespoon parsley
¼ teaspoon ground coriander
¼ teaspoon freshly grated nutmeg
a pinch of ground cumin
900ml (1½ pints) vegetable stock or water
750ml (1¼ pints) milk
1 teaspoon salt
freshly ground black pepper
25g (1oz) butter
100g (4oz) freshly grated Parmesan cheese

Heat the olive oil in a large saucepan and cook the pumpkin, potatoes and herbs over a moderate heat for 3 minutes. Add the spices and stock or water, bring to the boil, cover and simmer for 1 hour. Remove the bay leaf. Force the soup through a sieve or purée in a blender and return to the saucepan. Add the milk, salt and black pepper to taste and bring to the boil. Stir in the butter and serve with the grated cheese on the side.

Luguria   **PREBOGGION**   Serves 6
                   Preboggion

Preboggion are bunches of wild herbs and greens found in the region around Genoa. This delicious soup is rich in vitamins and minerals. Add as many different green leafy vegetables and herbs as you have on hand. The soup is thickened with rice and enriched with pesto sauce.

2 tablespoons olive oil
1 small onion
1 stalk celery, thinly sliced
a handful of parsley, chopped
1 tablespoon fresh marjoram, or ½ teaspoon dried

1 tablespoon fresh chives, chopped, or 1 teaspoon dried
¼ Savoy cabbage, shredded
100g (4oz) Swiss chard, shredded
100g (4oz) beet leaves, shredded
100g (4oz) spinach, shredded
1 bunch watercress, shredded
1.2 litres (2 pints) vegetable stock or water
175g (6oz) long grain rice
120ml (4fl oz) pesto sauce (see page 58)
salt
freshly ground black pepper
100g (4oz) freshly grated Pecorino Sardo or Parmesan
   cheese

Heat the olive oil in a large saucepan and cook the onion,
celery, parsley, marjoram and chives over a moderate heat
for 3 minutes. Add the Savoy cabbage, Swiss chard, beet
leaves, spinach, watercress and stock. Bring to the boil
and simmer for 30 minutes.

Increase the heat and when the soup is boiling add the
rice. Cook for 20 minutes or until the rice is tender but still
firm. Remove from the heat and stir in the pesto sauce.
Season to taste with salt and black pepper. Serve at once
with grated cheese on the side.

Lombardy   **RICE, PEA AND**   Serves 6
                  LETTUCE SOUP
           Minestra di riso, piselle e lattugha

This is a light and refreshing summer soup.

15g (½oz) butter
1 tablespoon olive oil
1.7 litres (3 pints) vegetable stock
250g (9oz) fresh peas, shelled
1 Webb's lettuce, shredded
175g (6oz) long grain rice
1 teaspoon salt
freshly ground black pepper
100g (4oz) freshly grated Parmesan cheese

Heat the butter and olive oil in a large saucepan. Add the stock and the peas, bring to the boil and cook for 20 minutes or until the peas are tender. Add the shredded lettuce and simmer for 10 minutes.

Increase the heat and when the soup is boiling add the rice. Season to taste with salt and black pepper. Cook for 20 minutes or until the rice is tender but still firm. Serve at once with the grated cheese on the side.

Friuli and Venezia Giulia   **RICE AND**   Serves 6
                                 LEMON SOUP
                                 Minestra di riso e limone

This refreshing summer soup has a Greek influence.

1.85 litres (3¼ pints) vegetable stock (see page 63)
175g (6oz) long grain rice
4 egg yolks
50g (2oz) freshly grated Parmesan cheese
juice of ½ lemon

Bring the stock to the boil in a large saucepan and pour in the rice. Beat the egg yolks with 2 tablespoons of the Parmesan cheese in a bowl. Slowly beat in the lemon juice in small drops. When the rice is tender but still firm, remove the pan from the heat and slowly mix a ladleful of hot soup into the egg mixture. Gradually pour the mixture back into the hot soup. Heat thoroughly and serve with the remaining Parmesan cheese on the side.

Sicily   **RICE AND LENTIL SOUP**   Serves 4 to 6
              Minestra di riso e lenticche

This is a warming, substantial soup that is rich in protein. Follow it with one of the lighter main courses, such as a cheese soufflé or stuffed courgettes with mushrooms. Use the small green lentils found in Italian groceries or deli-catessens.

225g (8oz) green lentils
3 tablespoons olive oil
2 garlic cloves, crushed
1 small onion, chopped
225g (8oz) canned plum tomatoes, seeded and chopped
salt
freshly ground black pepper
150g (5oz) long grain rice
50g (2oz) freshly grated Pecorino cheese

Wash the lentils carefully and bring to the boil in 1.2 litres (2 pints) water. Cover and simmer for 1½ hours or until they are tender.

Heat the olive oil in a large saucepan and cook the garlic and onion over a moderate heat for 3 minutes. Add the chopped tomatoes and cook over a high heat for 5 minutes. Add the lentils and their cooking liquid, salt, black pepper and enough water to make up to 1.85 litres (3¼ pints). Bring to the boil and simmer for 30 minutes. Increase the heat and when the soup is boiling, pour in the rice. Cook for 20 minutes or until the rice is tender but still firm. Serve at once with the grated cheese on the side.

Valle d'Aosta **CABBAGE AND** Serves 6
FONTINA CHEESE SOUP
Zuppa alla valpelleunenze

This is a cross between a soup and a casserole. Layers of bread, cabbage and Fontina cheese are arranged in a large casserole and bathed in stock. The 'soup' is then baked in the oven until the cabbage is very tender and the top is nicely browned.

1 small green cabbage
12 slices French bread, about 1cm (½ inch) thick
175g (6oz) Fontina cheese, thinly sliced
1.85 litres (3¼ pints) hot vegetable stock (see page 00)
75g (3oz) freshly grated Parmesan cheese
50g (2oz) butter, melted

Wash the cabbage, discard the tough outer leaves, and cut the head into quarters. Steam for 7 minutes or until tender. Allow to cool and chop finely.

Place the French bread in a single layer in a large casserole. Cover with chopped cabbage and top with slices of Fontina cheese. Pour over the hot stock and sprinkle with grated Parmesan cheese. Dribble melted butter over the top. Bake in a preheated oven at 160°C (325°F/Gas Mark 3) for 1 hour or until the cabbage is very soft and the top is lightly browned. Serve at once.

Piedmont   **GARDEN VEGETABLE**   Serves 4 to 6
                      SOUP
                 Minestra giardiniera

This is a simple, light vegetable soup using early summer vegetables. No pasta, rice or bread is used to thicken this soup.

15g (½oz) butter
2 tablespoons olive oil
1 garlic clove, crushed
1 leek, thinly sliced
2 carrots, diced
1 turnip, diced
2 small potatoes, peeled and diced
1.2 litres (2 pints) vegetable stock or water
175 ml (6oz) fresh peas, shelled
1 Webb's lettuce, shredded
salt
freshly ground black pepper
100g (4oz) freshly grated Parmesan cheese

Heat the butter and olive oil in a large saucepan and cook the garlic, leek, carrots, turnip and potatoes over a moderate heat for 5 minutes.

Add the stock or water, peas, lettuce and salt and black pepper to taste. Bring to the boil and simmer for 30 minutes or until the vegetables are tender. Serve with the grated cheese on the side.

Valle d'Aosta   **ALPINE SPLIT**   Serves 6
                     PEA SOUP
                 Crema di verdure passati

175g (6oz) dried split peas
1.2 litres (2 pints) vegetable stock (see page 63)
2 tablespoons olive oil
1 large onion, thinly sliced
2 carrots, diced
1 turnip, diced
1 leek, thinly sliced
2 medium potatoes, diced
1 bay leaf
120ml (4fl oz) single cream
1 teaspoon salt
freshly ground black pepper
6 slices of wholemeal bread, cut into small squares

Soak the split peas in water overnight and drain. Bring to
the boil in the stock and simmer for 1½ hours or until the
split peas are tender.

Heat the olive oil in a large saucepan and cook the
onion, carrots, turnip, leek, potatoes and bay leaf over a
moderate heat for 5 minutes. Add the split peas and their
cooking liquid, cover and simmer for 20 minutes.

After removing the bay leaf, force the soup through a
sieve or purée in a blender and return to the saucepan. If
the mixture is too thick, thin with a little boiling water.

Stir the cream into the soup and add salt and black
pepper to taste. Dry the squares of bread in a 190°C
(375°F/Gas Mark 5) oven until golden to make croûtons.
Heat the soup thoroughly and serve with croûtons.

Veneto   **PASTA AND BEAN SOUP**   Serves 6
                     Pasta e fasoi

This is a classic Venetian soup made with the famous
white beans from Lamon. Cannelini or small white beans

may be used instead. Like many Tuscan bean soups, half of the cooked beans are puréed and used to thicken the soup.

350g (12oz) dried white haricot beans
65ml (2½fl oz) olive oil
2 garlic cloves, crushed
1 small onion, chopped
1 stalk celery, thinly sliced
a handful of parsley, finely chopped
1 bay leaf
100g (4oz) canned plum tomatoes, forced through a sieve or
  puréed in a food processor
1.85 litres (3¼ pints) vegetable stock (see page 63)
225g (8oz) egg noodles
50g (2oz) freshly grated Parmesan cheese

Soak the beans in water overnight and drain.

Heat the olive oil in a large saucepan and cook the garlic, onion, celery, parsley and bay leaf for 2 minutes. Add the puréed tomatoes, drained beans and stock. Bring slowly to the boil and cook for 1½ to 2 hours or until the beans are tender. Remove the bay leaf. Purée half of the beans and vegetables and return to the saucepan. The soup should have the consistency of thin cream; if it is too thick, thin it with a little water. Bring slowly to the boil and simmer for 5 minutes.

Increase the heat. When the soup is boiling drop in the egg noodles and cook until they are tender but still firm. Serve with the grated cheese on the side.

Friuli and **BEAN AND** Serves 4
Venezia Giulia **BARLEY SOUP** to 6
Minestra di fagioli e orzo

175g (6oz) dried borlotti beans
150g (5oz) pearl barley
1.85 litres (3¼ pints) water

3 tablespoons olive oil
2 garlic cloves, crushed
1 stalk celery, diced
1 carrot, diced
1 small bunch parsley, finely chopped
1 bay leaf
¼ teaspoon ground cumin
salt
freshly ground black pepper
100g (4oz) freshly grated Parmesan cheese

Soak the beans in water overnight and drain. Bring to the boil in the water with the barley. Cover and simmer for 2 hours or until the beans and barley are tender.

Heat the olive oil in a large saucepan and cook the garlic, celery, carrot, parsley, bay leaf and cumin over a moderate heat for 3 minutes. Add the beans and barley and their cooking liquid. Season to taste with salt and black pepper. Simmer for 30 minutes or until the celery and carrot are tender. Serve hot with the grated cheese on the side.

Piedmont   **CHICK PEA AND**   Serves 6
                  TURNIP SOUP
                      Cisrá

350g (12oz) dried chick peas
2 litres (3½ pints) water
3 tablespoons olive oil
1 garlic clove, crushed
1 small onion, chopped
2 turnips, diced
1 stalk celery, thinly sliced
225oz (8oz) turnip tops, coarsely chopped
salt
freshly ground black pepper
6 slices of wholemeal bread, cut into small squares
100g (4oz) freshly grated Parmesan cheese

Soak the chick peas in water overnight and drain. Bring to the boil in the water and cook for 2½ to 3 hours or until the chick peas are tender.

Heat the olive oil in a large saucepan and cook the garlic, onion, turnips and celery over a moderate heat for 8 to 10 minutes until the vegetables are tender and starting to turn golden. Add the chick peas and their cooking liquid, turnip tops, salt and black pepper to taste and simmer for a further 30 minutes. Dry the squares of bread in a 190°C (375°F/Gas Mark 5) oven until golden to make croûtons.

Place the croûtons in individual soup bowls and pour over the soup. Serve with the grated cheese on the side.

Emilia-   **COURGETTE SOUP**   Serves 6
Romagna   *Zuppa di zucchine*

2 tablespoons olive oil
1 small onion
1 bay leaf
2 tablespoons fresh parsley, chopped
1 teaspoon fresh basil leaves, or ¼ teaspoon dried

450g (1 lb) courgettes, thinly sliced
1.85 litres (3¼ pints) hot vegetable stock (see page 63)
⅛ teaspoon freshly grated nutmeg
2 eggs
100g (4oz) freshly grated Parmesan cheese
6 slices of wholemeal bread, cut into small squares

Heat the olive oil in a saucepan and cook the onion and herbs for 3 minutes. Add the courgettes and hot stock. Bring to the boil, cover and simmer for 25 minutes or until the courgettes are tender.

Force the soup through a sieve or purée in a blender and return to the saucepan. Add the nutmeg. Beat the eggs with half the grated cheese in a bowl. Gradually mix a ladleful of hot soup into the eggs, then slowly stir the mixture back into the soup. Heat through but do not boil. Dry the squares of bread in a 190°C (375°F/Gas Mark 5) oven until golden to make croûtons.

Place the croûtons in individual soup bowls and pour over the soup. Serve at once with the grated cheese on the side.

Tuscany **TUSCAN MINESTRONE** Serves 5
SOUP to 6
Minestrone alla Toscana

The most important ingredient of Tuscan minestrone soup is the dried beans. Usually all or part of the cooked beans are puréed before they are added to the soup. Either rice or pasta may be used as an additional thickener.

175g (6oz) dried white cannelini beans
1.7 litres (3 pints) water
3 tablespoons olive oil
2 garlic cloves, crushed
1 small onion, chopped
1 stalk celery, thinly sliced
1 leek, thinly sliced
a pinch of rosemary

a pinch of thyme
a handful of parsley, chopped
1 bunch kale, shredded
1 curly endive, shredded
225g (8oz) canned plum tomatoes, forced through a sieve or
*   puréed in a food processor*
75g (3oz) elbow macaroni
100g (4oz) freshly grated Parmesan cheese

Soak the dried beans in water overnight and drain. Bring
to the boil in the water, cover and simmer for 1½ hours or
until the beans are tender. Force the beans and the cooking
liquid through a sieve or purée in a blender. Set aside.

Heat the olive oil in a large saucepan and cook the
garlic, onion, celery, leek and herbs over a moderate heat
for 3 minutes. Add the kale and cook for a further 5
minutes. Stir in the puréed tomatoes and the bean purée,
adding a little more water if the soup is too thick. Bring
slowly to the boil, cover and simmer for 15 minutes.

Increase the heat. When the soup is boiling, drop in the
elbow macaroni and cook until it is tender but still firm.
Serve at once with the grated cheese on the side.

Liguria   **MINESTRONE SOUP**   Serves 6
WITH PESTO
Minestrone con pesto

The selection of vegetables used in minestrone soup varies
from region to region. In Liguria, a typical minestrone
soup consists of broad beans, courgettes, French beans,
peas and potatoes. Aubergine and cardoons are sometimes
included. What makes a Ligurian minestrone unique is the
addition of the famous *pesto* sauce. Either pasta or rice
may be used as an additional thickener.

50ml (2fl oz) olive oil
2 garlic cloves, crushed
1 onion, chopped
1 stalk celery, thinly sliced

a handful of parsley, chopped
2 courgettes, diced
175g (6oz) French beans, cut into 2.5cm (1 inch) lengths
175g (6oz) fresh broad beans, shelled
175g (6oz) shelled fresh peas
2 potatoes, diced
¼ Savoy cabbage, shredded
450g (1 lb) Swiss chard, shredded
1.7 litres (3 pints) water
225g (8oz) egg noodles, broken into 5cm (2 inch) lengths
250ml (8fl oz) pesto sauce (see page 58)
100g (4oz) freshly grated Parmesan cheese

Heat the olive oil in a large saucepan and cook the garlic, onion, celery and parsley over a moderate heat for 3 minutes. Add the courgettes, French beans, broad beans, peas, potatoes, cabbage, Swiss chard and water. Bring to the boil, cover and simmer for 1½ hours.

Increase the heat. When the soup is boiling, drop in the egg noodles and cook until tender but still firm. Remove from the heat. Stir in the pesto sauce and serve at once with the grated cheese on the side.

Apulia   **GREEN MINESTRONE**   Serves 6
Minestrone verde alla barese

This is a speciality of Bari. The green vegetables may be varied according to what is in season. Cabbage, spinach, kale, and watercress all make excellent variations.

3 tablespoons olive oil
2 garlic cloves, crushed
1 onion, chopped
1 fennel bulb, diced
1 carrot, diced
2 stalks celery, thinly sliced
450g (1 lb) potatoes, diced
1 bunch Swiss chard, shredded
225g (8oz) spring greens, coarsely chopped

225g (8oz) beet leaves, shredded
225g (8oz) turnip tops, shredded
1.85 litres (3¼ pints) vegetable stock or water
1 bay leaf
a pinch of ground cloves
salt
freshly ground black pepper
225g (8oz) spaghetti, broken into 5cm (2 inch) lengths
100g (4oz) freshly grated Parmesan cheese

Heat the olive oil in a large saucepan and cook the garlic, onion, fennel, carrot and celery over a moderate heat for 5 minutes. Add the potatoes, Swiss chard, spring greens, beet leaves and turnip tops and continue to cook for 5 minutes. Add the stock, the bay leaf and cloves. Season with salt and pepper to taste. Bring to the boil, cover and simmer for 1 hour. Increase the heat and when the soup is boiling add the spaghetti and cook until it is tender but still firm. Serve with the grated cheese on the side.

Calabria   **MILLECOSEDDE**   Serves 6
Millecosedde

Millecosedde means 'a thousand little things'. All the odds and ends of pasta, dried beans and vegetables can be used up in this recipe.

75g (3oz) dried white haricot beans
75g (3oz) chick peas
75g (3oz) green lentils
1.85 litres (3¼ pints) water
3 tablespoons olive oil
2 garlic cloves, crushed
1 onion, chopped
1 carrot, diced
2 stalks celery, thinly sliced
1 turnip, diced
1 potato, diced
a handful of parsley, chopped

1 teaspoon fresh oregano, or ¼ teaspoon dried
1 bay leaf
100g (4oz) mushrooms, sliced
1 bunch beet leaves or spinach, shredded
1 bunch collards or kale, shredded
salt
freshly ground black pepper
225g (8oz) spaghetti, broken into 5cm (2 inch) lengths
100g (4oz) freshly grated Pecorino cheese

Soak the dried vegetables overnight and drain. Bring to the boil in the water and simmer for 2 hours or until all the dried vegetables are tender. Drain and reserve the cooking liquid.

Heat the olive oil in a large saucepan and cook the garlic, onion, carrot, celery, turnip, potato, parsley and oregano over a moderate heat for 5 minutes. Add the bay leaf, mushrooms, beet leaves and collards and cook for a further 5 minutes. Add the reserved cooking liquid and salt and black pepper to taste. Bring to the boil and simmer for 1 hour.

Add the drained dried vegetables and a little more water if the soup is too thick. Increase the heat. When the soup is boiling, add the spaghetti and cook until it is tender but still firm. Serve with the grated cheese on the side.

GRAINS

BREAD
Pane

Bread is still the staff of life in Italy, especially in the poorer regions of the south. Although most people think of Italian bread as white and crusty, similar to French bread, darker more solid bread can be found.

In this chapter you will find recipes for two of these darker, more nutritious loaves. One is a firm, close-grained barley bread from Lombardy; the other is *pane integrale*, a lighter, softer wholemeal bread that is made all over Italy.

Lombardy **BARLEY BREAD** Serves 6
Brazadel

Brazadel is a delicious, crusty barley bread found in the Valtellina Valley. The grain is coarse and greyish and keeps very well.

21 g (³⁄₄oz) active dry yeast
450 ml (³⁄₄ pint) warm water
2 tablespoons honey
300 g (10 oz) barley flour
300 g (10 oz) wholemeal flour
300 g (10 oz) strong white flour
2 teaspoons salt
2 tablespoons olive oil

Dissolve the yeast in the warm water in a large mixing bowl. Stir in the honey and leave for 5 minutes until the yeast is creamy.

Place the barley, wholemeal and white flours and salt in a bowl and blend well together. Add half the flour mixture to the yeast and beat together with a wooden spoon for 10 minutes to incorporate plenty of air into the dough, which should have the consistency of thick mud. Cover the bowl with cling film and leave in a warm place for 1 hour until the dough has doubled in bulk.

Knock the dough down and carefully fold in the olive oil and 50 g (2 oz) flour. Gradually fold in more flour until the dough starts to come away from the sides of the bowl. Place the dough on a lightly floured work surface and knead well for 10 minutes. Add more flour as necessary.

Place the dough in a lightly greased mixing bowl. Cover with cling film and leave in a warm place until the dough has doubled in bulk. (If you are in a hurry you may omit the second rising, but the bread will be a little heavier.)

Knock the dough down, place on a lightly floured work surface and shape into two round domed loaves. Cut a cross in the centre of each loaf and place on a greased baking sheet. Bake in a preheated oven at 180°C (350°F/ Gas Mark 4) for about 50 minutes. When the bread is done, it will sound slightly hollow when tapped on the under-side. Cool thoroughly on a wire rack before eating.

All Italy **WHOLEMEAL BREAD** Makes 2
Pane integrale   loaves

Pane integrale or wholemeal bread is found in most regions of Italy. Wholemeal flour is combined with white flour in equal proportions to make a softer, lighter loaf than the usual wholemeal bread.

21 g (¾oz) active dry yeast
450 ml (¾ pint) warm water
2 tablespoons honey
425 g (15 oz) wholemeal flour
425 g (15 oz) strong white flour
3 teaspoons salt
2 tablespoons olive oil

Follow the same directions as for barley bread on page 82. After the second rising, knock the dough down. Place on a lightly floured work surface and shape into two round domed loaves. Cut a cross in the centre of each loaf.

Place the loaves on a greased baking sheet. Bake in a preheated oven at 180°C (350°F/Gas Mark 4) for about 50 minutes. When the bread is done it will sound slightly hollow when tapped on the under-side. Cool thoroughly on a wire rack before eating.

FLAT BREAD
Foccaccia

Foccaccia, or flat bread is a descendant of the ancient hearth cake that the Romans introduced around Europe. The dough was baked on hearthstones under the ashes of the fire, producing ashcakes or *foccaccie*.

Foccaccia is primarily made in northern Italy and is the forerunner of the pizza that is made in the south. Today, *foccaccie* are leavened with yeast and baked in the oven. There are many versions, some of which are flavoured very simply with rosemary or sage, while some are studded with olives and others topped with onions or sun-dried tomatoes.

Foccaccie are easy to make. The exact thickness of the dough depends on your preference. They may be made 1 cm (½ inch) thick, which produces a crisp, cracker-like crust, or they may be made up to 5 cm (2 inch) thick, which is more like a bread.

Emilia-Romagna   **FLAT BREAD**   Serves 4
WITH OLIVES
Foccaccia con olive

15g (½oz) active dry yeast
250 ml (8 fl oz) warm water
450–550g (1–1¼lb) wholemeal or plain white flour
5 tablespoons olive oil
175g (6oz) black Italian or Greek olives, stoned and sliced
1 teaspoon salt
a little cornmeal

Dissolve the yeast in the warm water in a large mixing bowl. Allow to stand for 10 minutes until the yeast is dissolved and the mixture is light beige in colour and creamy. Fold in 225g (8oz) flour and beat until the dough forms a sticky mass. Sprinkle some of the remaining flour on a work surface or large board and turn out the sticky dough on to the board. Gradually knead in the remaining flour until the dough is smooth and elastic and no longer sticks to your hands.

Place the dough in an oiled bowl, cover with cling film and leave in a warm place for 1 hour until the dough has risen and doubled in bulk. Knock the dough down carefully and fold in 4 tablespoons of olive oil, the sliced olives and salt. Place on the floured work surface and knead again until smooth. Roll the dough out to a circle about 25–30 cm (10–12 inches) in diameter.

Place on a well-greased 38 cm (15 inch) pizza pan that has been dusted with cornmeal. Brush the top of the *foccaccia* with the remaining tablespoon of olive oil and leave to rise in the pan for 1 hour or until doubled in bulk. Bake in a preheated oven at 200°C (400°F/Gas Mark 6) for 30 minutes or until the top is golden. For a thinner, crisper *foccaccia*, roll the dough out to a 38 cm (15 inch) circle and bake for 20 minutes.

Lombardy   **ONION FOCCACCIA**   Serves 4
Foccaccia con cipolle

250 ml (8 fl oz) warm water
15 g (½ oz) active dry yeast
450–550 g (1–1¼ lb) wholemeal or plain white flour
1 teaspoon salt
6 tablespoons olive oil
a little cornmeal
450 g (1 lb) Spanish onions, thinly sliced
freshly ground black pepper

Follow the directions for flat bread with olives on page 84. After the dough has doubled in bulk, knock it down and carefully fold in 4 tablespoons olive oil and the salt. Place on the work surface and knead again until smooth. Roll the dough out to a circle about 25–30 cm (10–12 inches) in diameter, or flatten it into shape with your hands. Any indentations on the surface will help to hold the topping. Place the *foccaccia* on a well-greased 38 cm (15 inch) pizza pan that has been dusted with cornmeal. Allow to rise for 1 hour.

Heat the remaining olive oil in a frying pan and gently cook the onions for 8 to 10 minutes or until they are translucent. Spread the onions over the risen dough and sprinkle with black pepper. Bake in a preheated oven at 220°C (425°F/Gas Mark 7) for 30 minutes or until the bread is golden.

PIZZA, CALZONE
AND PANZAROTTI
Pizza, Calzone e Panzarotti

'Bread with a relish' was a favourite snack of both the
Romans and the ancient Greeks. The relish might have
consisted of olive oil, herbs, wine, spices, olives or cheese.
It was the Greeks who first conceived of baking the relish
together with the bread and so created the forerunner of
pizza as we know it today.

The Neapolitans transformed this poor man's dish into
a medley of bread, vegetables, herbs and cheese. The
tomato was introduced into Neapolitan cooking in the
eighteenth century, but it was not until 1889 that the
classic pizza of tomatoes, cheese, olive oil and herbs was
invented in commemoration of the Italian flag and named
in honour of Queen Margherita, who was an avid pizza
lover.

Pizza literally means 'pie'. Many versions of pizza are
found all over Italy. Some are double-crust pies, like *pizza
alla perugina*, which has a simple filling of Gruyère cheese.
Others are more like a bread, such as the cheese-flavoured
pizza di formaggio from Ancona.

Another favourite form of pizza is the *calzone* which
literally means 'trouser leg'. It is simply a folded pizza that
has been stuffed with a pizza topping then baked in the
oven or possibly deep-fried.

Panzarotti is an even smaller relative of *calzone*. It is a
stuffed turnover of 5 to 7.5 cm (2 to 3 inches) in length
made of pastry or pasta dough and then baked in the oven
or deep-fried until crisp and golden.

PIZZA DOUGH

15 g (½oz) active dry yeast
250 ml (8 fl oz) warm water
*425 g (15 oz) wholemeal or plain white flour or half plain
white and half wholemeal flour, sifted with ½ teaspoon
salt*

Mix the yeast with warm water in a large mixing bowl. Allow it to stand for 10 minutes until the yeast is dissolved and is light beige in colour and creamy.

Fold in 225g (8oz) flour and beat until the dough forms a sticky mass. Sprinkle some of the remaining flour on a work surface or large board and gradually knead in the remaining flour until the dough is smooth and elastic and no longer sticks to your hands. Cover with cling film and allow to rise in a warm place for about 1 hour or until doubled in bulk.

Knock the dough down and place it on the floured work surface. Knead briefly and roll out into a 38cm (15 inch) circle, no more than 5mm (¼ inch) thick. Place in a well-greased pizza pan and top with the topping of your choice.

Campania   **PIZZA MARGHERITA**   Serves 4
Pizza Margherita

This is a classic pizza with a topping of Mozzarella cheese, tomatoes, olive oil and herbs. Canned plum tomatoes may be used instead of fresh tomatoes.

1 recipe pizza dough (see above)
a little cornmeal
225g (8oz) ripe plum tomatoes, peeled, seeded and chopped
3 tablespoons olive oil
2 teaspoons fresh basil, or ½ teaspoon dried
1 teaspoon fresh oregano, or ¼ teaspoon dried
225g (8oz) Mozzarella cheese, sliced

Roll out the pizza dough to a circle 38cm (15 inches) in diameter. Place in a well-greased pizza pan that has been dusted with cornmeal. Allow to rise in a warm place for 1 hour or until the dough has doubled in bulk.

Drain the chopped tomatoes. Heat 1 tablespoon of olive oil in a frying pan and cook the tomatoes over a moderate heat for 5 minutes. Spread them over the pizza, sprinkle with basil and oregano and top with slices of Mozzarella cheese. Dribble the remaining olive oil over the top. Bake in a preheated oven at 230°C (450°F/Gas Mark 8) for 15–20 minutes.

Campania **PIZZA WITH MUSHROOMS**   Serves 4
Pizza con funghi

1 recipe pizza dough (see page 86)
a little cornmeal
4 tablespoons olive oil
225g (8oz) canned plum tomatoes, drained
1 garlic clove, crushed
2 tablespoons parsley, finely chopped
1 teaspoon fresh oregano, or ½ teaspoon dried
450g (1lb) mushrooms, sliced
175g (6oz) Mozzarella cheese, sliced
3 tablespoons freshly grated Parmesan cheese

Roll out the pizza dough to a circle 38cm (15 inches) in diameter. Place in a well-greased pizza pan that has been dusted with cornmeal. Allow to rise in a warm place for 1 hour or until doubled in bulk.

Heat 1 tablespoon olive oil in a frying pan and cook the tomatoes over a moderate heat for 5 minutes. Spread over the pizza. Drain the tomatoes and chop.

Heat 1 tablespoon olive oil in another frying pan and cook the garlic, parsley and oregano for 1 minute. Add the mushrooms and cook over a moderate heat for 5 minutes or until they are tender.

Spoon the mushrooms over the tomatoes, top with slices of Mozzarella cheese and sprinkle with Parmesan cheese. Dribble over the remaining olive oil and bake in a preheated oven at 230°C (450°F/Gas Mark 8) oven for 15–20 minutes.

Apulia   **SWISS CHARD PIZZA**   Serves 4
Pizza di bietole

1 recipe pizza dough (see page 86)
a little cornmeal

900g (2lb) Swiss chard
2 tablespoons olive oil
2 garlic cloves, crushed
salt
freshly ground black pepper
225g (8oz) Mozzarella cheese, sliced
3 tablespoons freshly grated Pecorino cheese
16 Italian or Greek black olives

Roll out the pizza dough to a circle 38cm (15 inches) in diameter. Place in a well-greased pizza pan that has been dusted with cornmeal. Allow to rise in a warm place for 1 hour or until it has doubled in bulk.

Wash the Swiss chard, cut away the thick stalks and chop the leaves coarsely. Heat the olive oil in a saucepan and cook the garlic for 1 minute. Add the chopped leaves, cover and cook over a moderate heat for 5 minutes or until they are tender, stirring constantly so that the leaves cook evenly. Season to taste with salt and black pepper.

Spread the Swiss chard over the pizza. Top with slices of Mozzarella cheese, sprinkle with Pecorino cheese and garnish with black olives. Bake in a preheated oven at 230°C (450°F/Gas Mark 8) for 15–20 minutes.

Sicily **PIZZA WITH AUBERGINE** Serves 4
Pizza alla siciliana

1 recipe pizza dough (see page 86)
a little cornmeal
1 small aubergine (about 225g (8oz))
salt
65ml (2½fl oz) olive oil
250ml (8fl oz) tomato sauce (see page 54)
a pinch of hot red pepper flakes
175g (6oz) Caciocavallo or Mozzarella cheese, sliced
15 Italian or Greek black olives
1 tablespoon capers
3 tablespoons freshly grated Pecorino cheese

Roll out the pizza dough to a circle 38cm (15 inches) in diameter. Place in a well-greased pizza pan that has been dusted with cornmeal. Allow to rise in a warm place for 1 hour or until it has doubled in bulk.

Peel the aubergine and cut into slices about 3mm (⅛ inch) thick. Sprinkle with salt and set in a colander for 1 hour to release the bitter juices. Wash off the salt and pat the slices dry.

Heat 50ml (2fl oz) olive oil in a frying pan and quickly brown the aubergine on both sides. Drain on a paper towel.

Prepare the tomato sauce and add the hot red pepper flakes. Spread the sauce over the dough and cover with the fried aubergine slices. Top with Caciocavallo or Mozzarella cheese and dot with black olives and capers. Sprinkle the Pecorino cheese liberally over the top. Dribble over the remaining olive oil and bake in a preheated oven at 230°C (450°F/Gas Mark 8) for 15–20 minutes.

Calabria   **ONION PIE**   Serves 4
                      Pitta calabrese

In Calabria a stuffed pizza or pie is called a *pitta*. It is an Arab word. The dish dates back to the days when much of southern Italy was overrun by the Saracens.

4 tablespoons olive oil
1 teaspoon fresh oregano
900g (2lb) onions, thinly sliced
salt
freshly ground black pepper
1 recipe pizza dough (see page 86)
a little cornmeal
100g (4oz) Caciocavallo or Mozzarella cheese, sliced
25g (1oz) freshly grated Pecorino cheese

Heat 3 tablespoons of olive oil in a large frying pan and cook the oregano and onions over a low heat for 25 to 30 minutes or until the onions are very soft. Do not allow to brown. Sprinkle with salt and black pepper.

Divide the pizza dough in two, making one portion larger than the other. Roll out the larger piece to a thin 40cm (16 inch) circle and arrange on the bottom of a well-greased 38cm (15 inch) pizza pan that has been dusted with cornmeal. Spread the onions over the dough. Cover with slices of Caciocavallo or Mozzarella cheese and sprinkle with Pecorino cheese.

Roll out the second piece of dough to a 35cm (14 inch) circle and place it over the filling. Fold the bottom rim over the top layer of dough and press with a fork all around the pitta to seal in the filling. Brush the top with the remaining olive oil. Bake in a preheated oven at 230°C (450°F/Gas Mark 8) for 30 to 40 minutes or until the top is golden.

Umbria   **CHEESE PIE**   Serves 4
Pizza alla perugina

This is a double-crust pizza with a simple filling of Gruyère cheese. Melted butter and milk are added to the dough to make the crust softer and richer than that of a standard pizza.

15g (½oz) active dry yeast
250ml (8fl oz) warm milk

425g (13oz) plain white flour
½ teaspoon salt
120ml (4fl oz) melted butter
225g (8oz) Gruyère cheese, thinly sliced
1 egg yolk
2 tablespoons cold water

Mix the yeast with the warm milk in a large mixing bowl. Allow to stand for 10 minutes until the yeast is dissolved and the mixture is light beige in colour and creamy. Fold in 300g (10oz) flour and beat until the dough forms a sticky mass.

Sprinkle some of the remaining flour on a work surface or large board and turn the sticky dough out on to it. Gradually knead in the remaining flour until the dough is smooth and elastic. Place in an oiled bowl and cover with cling film. Allow to rise in a warm place for 50 to 60 minutes or until the dough has doubled in bulk.

Knock the dough down and carefully fold in the salt and melted butter. Place on a floured work surface and knead again until smooth. Divide the dough in two, making one portion slightly larger than the other. Roll out the larger piece to a circle 35cm (14 inches) in diameter and arrange over the bottom of a well-greased pizza pan. Cover with slices of Gruyère cheese, leaving a 5cm (2 inch) border all around.

Roll out the second piece of dough to a 30cm (12 inch) circle and place it over the cheese filling. Fold the bottom rim over the top edge and press the two layers of dough with a fork. Brush the top lightly with egg yolk mixed with the water. Bake in a preheated oven at 230°C (450°F/Gas Mark 8) for 30 to 40 minutes or until the top is golden.

Le Marche   **CHEESE BREAD**   Serves 4 to 6
                Pizza con formaggio all'anconetana

This is a speciality of Ancona.

15g (½oz) active dry yeast
250ml (8fl oz) warm water

about 425g (15oz) plain white flour
2 eggs
2 tablespoons olive oil
50g (2oz) freshly grated Pecorino cheese
75g (3oz) Gruyère cheese, cut into small dice
½ teaspoon salt

Dissolve the yeast in the warm water in a large mixing bowl. Allow to stand for 10 minutes until the yeast is dissolved and the mixture is light in colour and creamy.

Fold in 300g (10oz) flour and beat until the dough forms a sticky mass. Cover the bowl with cling film and leave in a warm place for 1 hour or until the dough has risen and doubled in bulk.

Beat the eggs, olive oil, cheeses and salt together and beat into the risen dough. Sprinkle some of the remaining flour on to a work surface or large board and turn the sticky dough out on to it. Gradually knead in the remaining flour until the dough is smooth and elastic and no longer sticks to your hands. Place in a well-greased loaf tin. Cover with cling film and leave in a warm place to rise for 1½ hours or until doubled in bulk. Put in a preheated oven at 190°C (375°F/Gas Mark 5) and bake for 35 to 40 minutes or until the top is golden.

Campania   **CALZONI WITH**   Serves 6
THREE CHEESES
Calzoni a tre formaggii

1 recipe pizza dough (see page 86)
350g (12oz) Ricotta cheese
1 whole egg
1 egg yolk
225g (8oz) Mozzarella cheese, cut into small dice
50g (2oz) freshly grated Parmesan cheese
salt
freshly ground black pepper
1 egg yolk beaten with 1 tablespoon water

Divide the dough into six pieces and roll out each piece to a circle 20 cm (8 inches) in diameter.

Combine the Ricotta cheese, the whole egg, the egg yolk, Mozzarella and Parmesan cheeses, salt and black pepper in a bowl and blend well. Spoon the filling evenly on to the lower half of each circle. Brush the edges of the dough with a little of the egg yolk beaten with water. Fold over and crimp the edges securely together with a fork or your finger.

Carefully transfer each *calzone* with a spatula to a well-greased baking sheet. Brush the tops with the remaining beaten egg and allow to rise in a warm place for 30 minutes. Bake in a preheated oven at 230°C (450°F/Gas Mark 8) for 20–30 minutes or until the tops are golden.

Apulia	**VEGETABLE CALZONI**	Serves 6
	Calzoni con verdure alla barese	

This *calzone* is a speciality of Bari and has a deliciously piquant filling that is very typical of Apulian cooking.

1 recipe pizza dough (see page 86)
1 head curly endive (about 900 g (2 lb))
3 tablespoons olive oil
1 small onion, finely chopped
1 leek, thinly sliced
1 fennel bulb, cut into small dice
12 Italian or Greek black olives, stoned and sliced
1 tablespoon capers, coarsely chopped
salt
freshly ground black pepper
1 egg yolk, beaten

Divide the dough into six pieces and roll out each piece to a circle 20 cm (8 inches) in diameter.

Wash the endive and shred coarsely. Place in a covered saucepan and cook over a moderate heat for 5 minutes or until it is tender. The water clinging to the leaves is sufficient to prevent scorching. Drain and squeeze dry.

Heat the olive oil in a large frying pan and cook the onion, leek and fennel over a moderate heat for 7 minutes or until the fennel is just tender. Add the endive, olives and capers, with salt and black pepper to taste. Stir well and simmer for 5 minutes to mingle the flavours. Increase the heat at the end to evaporate any liquid.

Spoon the filling evenly on to half of each circle of dough. Brush the edges of the dough with the beaten egg. Fold over and crimp the edges together with a fork or your finger.

Carefully transfer each *calzone* with a spatula to a well-greased baking sheet. Brush the tops with the remaining beaten egg and bake in a preheated oven at 230°C (450°F/ Gas Mark 8) for 20 to 30 minutes or until the tops are golden.

Apulia   **CHEESE PANZAROTTI**   Serves 4
Panzarotti con uova e mozzarella   to 6

These delicious little cheese-filled pastries can be deep-fried or baked in the oven. They are found in Basilicata and Campania as well as Apulia.

1 recipe egg pasta dough (see page 98)
300g (10oz) Mozzarella cheese, sliced
40g (1½oz) freshly grated Parmesan cheese
3 eggs
2 tablespoons parsley, finely chopped
salt
freshly ground black pepper
2 tablespoons cold water
oil for deep-frying

Follow the directions for egg pasta on page 98. Allow the dough to rest for 30 minutes. In a bowl combine the Mozzarella and Parmesan cheese, 2 eggs and parsley with salt and black pepper to taste and mix well together.

Divide the dough in two and roll out to two thin sheets. Place scant teaspoonfuls of the filling over one sheet of the dough at regular intervals about 4cm (1½ inches) apart. Brush the other sheet of dough with the remaining egg, beaten with the water. Place this over the first sheet of dough and press well around each mound. Cut the *panzar-otti* into 4cm (1½ inch) squares with a pastry or ravioli cutter. Deep-fry in hot oil until crisp and golden on both sides. Drain on a paper towel and serve at once.

If you prefer, the *panzarotti* may be brushed lightly with beaten egg or olive oil and baked in a preheated oven at 230°C (450°F/Gas Mark 8) for 15 minutes.

PASTA
Pasta

Pasta falls into four categories. *Pasta secca* is a dry, factory-made pasta consisting of flour and water. Contrary to most people's belief, commercial pasta is not a devitalized food, especially when it is made from 100 per cent durum semolina. This has had only the bran removed and still contains most of the germ of the wheat. *Pasta all'uovo* is fresh home-made pasta enriched with eggs. The proportion is roughly 1 egg to 100g (4oz) flour, but this varies slightly from region to region. Milanese pasta uses 1 egg plus 1 yolk to 100g (4oz) flour. If more than 125g (4½oz) flour is used per egg, the dough will become dry and hard to handle. *Pasta ripiena* is stuffed pasta, usually home-made but sometimes made of dried pasta. *Pasta al forno* is baked pasta, which can be made of dried or fresh pasta.

To cook pasta
Use a minimum of 3.7 litres (7 pints) water to 450g (1lb) pasta. Add 1 tablespoon salt and 1 tablespoon olive oil to prevent the pasta from sticking together. Bring the water to the boil and keep at a rolling boil throughout cooking. Always stir with a wooden spoon as this helps to separate the strands of pasta.

The only way to test pasta to see if it is cooked is to taste it. It should be cooked *al dente,* which means still firm to the bite. Do not overcook it – nothing is worse than a bowl of mushy pasta.

Drain the cooked pasta in a colander or sieve and shake out any excess moisture. The pasta may be transferred to a heated serving bowl and tossed with sauce, or it may be heaped directly into individual soup bowls and topped with sauce. This is usually how it is served in Italy.

Sauces
As a general rule, the finer pastas are served with delicate sauces and the heavier pastas with more substantial sauces.

Cheeses
However perfectly you prepare the pasta and sauce, if you serve it with inferior cheese the result will be inferior. Always buy a fresh hunk of cheese and grate it just before

using. Parmesan, Pecorino Sardo, Pecorino Romano and Asiago are all excellent cheeses for grating.

Proportions for pasta dough

3 eggs 300 g (10 oz) flour ½ teaspoon salt	4 eggs 400 g (14 oz) flour ½ teaspoon salt	5 eggs 500 g (18 oz) flour 1 teaspoon salt

Widths of pasta

Tagliarini	3 mm (⅛ inch) wide
Fettucine or Tagliatelle	5 mm (¼ inch) wide
Trenette	1 cm (½ inch) wide
Pappardelle	2 cm (¾ inch) wide
Lasagne	5 cm (2 inches) wide by 15 cm (6 inches) long

Emilia-Romagna   **EGG PASTA**   Serves 4
                         La Sfoglia

Fresh egg pasta is usually made with semolina flour or unbleached plain white four, or a combination of both. If you prefer, you can use a mixture of wholemeal and plain white flour.

300 g (10 oz) semolina flour or plain white flour
3 eggs
½ teaspoon salt

Place the flour in a mound on a large wooden board on the table and form a deep well in the centre. Drop in 1 egg at a time and add the salt. Gradually beat in the flour with a fork, then form into a soft ball. Knead the dough well for 8 to 10 minutes or until it is smooth and elastic. Do not add too much flour or the dough will become hard to roll. If the dough is too dry, add a teaspoon or so of water.

Wrap the dough in a damp cloth and allow it to rest for

30 minutes. Divide the dough into four. Keep three parts of the dough wrapped. With a long thin rolling pin, roll out the remaining quarter of dough quickly, making quarter turns to form a circle. Speed is important as the dough will cease to be pliable as it dries out. When the dough is very thin and even, allow it to dry for 15 to 20 minutes – this will prevent the dough from sticking when it is rolled up – and cut it into noodles of the desired width. Repeat with the remaining portions of dough, keeping the pieces wrapped until ready to be rolled.

| Emilia- | **SPINACH PASTA** | Serves 4 |
| Romagna | *Pasta verde* | |

Pasta verde or green pasta can be made equally well with spinach, Swiss chard or beet leaves. In some regions of Italy young nettles or mint are included. In Liguria, green pasta is often made with borage instead of spinach.

225g (8oz) spinach
400g (14oz) semolina flour or plain white flour
2 eggs
½ teaspoon salt

Wash the spinach and cook in a covered saucepan for 5 minutes until it is tender. The water clinging to the leaves is sufficient to prevent scorching. Squeeze dry and chop very finely.

Place the flour in a mound on a large wooden board or table and form a deep well in the centre. Drop in 1 egg at a time followed by the spinach and salt. Gradually beat in the flour with a fork. Knead well for 8 to 10 minutes and proceed as for egg pasta on page 98.

Lombardy	**SAFFRON PASTA**	Serves 4
	WITH ONION SAUCE	
	La rechta con salsa di cipolle	

Milanese pasta dough contains more egg yolks than any other region of Italy.

Dough

300g (10oz) flour
2 eggs plus 2 egg yolks
½ teaspoon salt
1 teaspoon powdered saffron

Sauce

40g (1½oz) butter
2 tablespoons olive oil
3 Spanish onions, finely chopped
2 tablespoons fresh parsley, finely chopped
100g (4oz) canned plum tomatoes, forced through a sieve or
*   puréed in a food processor*
salt
freshly ground black pepper
100g (4oz) freshly grated Parmesan cheese

Follow the directions for egg pasta on page 98, using 2 eggs plus 2 yolks instead of 3 eggs. Beat the powdered saffron with the eggs before mixing them with the flour.

While the dough is resting, prepare the sauce. Heat 15g (½oz) butter and the olive oil in a large frying pan and cook the onions and parsley over a low heat for 30 minutes or until they are almost reduced to a purée. Do not allow to brown. Add the puréed tomatoes and cook over a moderate heat for 5 minutes, or until the sauce is thickened. Season with salt and black pepper to taste.

Roll out the dough to two very thin sheets and allow it to dry out for 10 minutes. If the dough is too moist, it will stick to itself when it is rolled out for cutting. Fold each sheet back and forth over itself three or four times. Cut into noodles 5mm (¼ inch) thick. Cook the noodles in plenty of lightly salted, boiling water until tender but still firm. Transfer to a heated serving bowl, dot with the remaining butter and pour over the sauce. Toss lightly and serve at once with the grated cheese on the side.

Liguria **TRENETTE WITH** Serves 4
PESTO SAUCE
Trenette con pesto

Trenette are fresh egg noodles cut into lengths 1 cm (½ inch) wide. The noodles are cooked together with potatoes and French beans and then dressed with pesto sauce.

Dough
300 g (10 oz) flour
3 eggs
½ teaspoon salt

Sauce
50 g (2 oz) fresh basil
2 garlic cloves, crushed
2 tablespoons olive oil
1 tablespoon pine nuts
1-2 tablespoons hot water
2 tablespoons freshly grated Pecorino Sardo cheese
2 medium potatoes, peeled and diced
225 g (8 oz) French beans, cut into 5 cm (2 inch) lengths
25 g (1 oz) butter

Follow the directions for egg pasta on page 98. Roll out the dough very thinly and leave to dry for 15 minutes. Roll up and cut into 1 cm (½ inch) wide noodles. Unfold the trenette and spread them out on a large towel or cloth to dry.

Place the basil, garlic, olive oil and pine nuts in a blender and work in short bursts until the ingredients are chopped. Add 1 or 2 tablespoons of hot water and the grated cheese. Blend at high speed until the mixture is smooth and creamy.

Cook the potatoes and French beans in a large saucepan of lightly salted boiling water. When they are almost cooked, add the trenette and cook for 5 minutes or until the noodles are tender but still firm. Drain and transfer to a heated serving bowl. Dot with butter and pour over the sauce. Toss well and serve at once.

| Emilia-Romagna | **TORTELLI WITH SWISS CHARD AND RICOTTA STUFFING** | Serves 4 |

Tortelli d'erbette

Filling
450g (1lb) Swiss chard
225g (8oz) Ricotta cheese
1 egg
50g (2oz) freshly grated Parmesan cheese
¼ teaspoon freshly grated nutmeg
salt
freshly ground black pepper

Dough
225g (8oz) flour
3 eggs
½ teaspoon salt

Topping
25g (1oz) butter
175ml (6fl oz) double cream, brought just to the boil
75g (3oz) freshly grated Parmesan cheese

Wash the Swiss chard and cook in a covered saucepan over a moderate heat for 5 minutes. The water clinging to the leaves is sufficient to prevent scorching. Squeeze it dry and chop coarsely.

Combine the chopped chard with the Ricotta cheese, egg, grated cheese and nutmeg with salt and black pepper to taste in a mixing bowl and blend well.

To make the dough, follow the directions for egg pasta on page 98. Allow the dough to rest and roll it out very thinly. Cut it into rounds about 5 cm (2 inches) in diameter. Place a scant teaspoon of filling in the centre of each round. Fold over the dough to form a half circle, then pick up the half circles and bend them around your index finger. Press the two ends together well to form a ring. Tortelli are said to resemble the navel of Venus which is a good guide to their finished shape. Line the tortelli up on a lightly floured board or tray and leave for 15 minutes to dry.

Cook the tortelli in plenty of lightly salted, boiling water for 5 to 6 minutes. Drain and transfer to a heated serving dish. Dot with butter and top with the hot cream and grated cheese. Toss lightly and serve at once.

Liguria and the North   **GREEN RAVIOLI WITH THREE CHEESES**   Serves 4
Ravioli verde a tre formaggii

Dough
325g (11oz) flour
2 eggs
225g (8oz) spinach
½ teaspoon salt

Filling
350g (12oz) Ricotta cheese
1 egg
50g (2oz) Mozzarella cheese, cut into small dice
50g (2oz) freshly grated Parmesan cheese
¼ teaspoon freshly grated nutmeg
salt
freshly ground black pepper

Sauce
350ml (17fl oz) mushroom and tomato sauce (see page 56)
25g (1oz) butter
100g (4oz) freshly grated Parmesan cheese

Follow the directions for spinach pasta on page 99. Roll the dough out to two very thin sheets. In a bowl, combine the Ricotta cheese, egg, Mozzarella and Parmesan cheeses and nutmeg with salt and black pepper to taste and blend well. Place teaspoonfuls of the filling over one sheet of the dough at regular intervals about 5cm (2 inches) apart. Cover with the other sheet of dough and press well around each mound.

Cut the ravioli into 5cm (2 inch) squares with a pastry or ravioli cutter. Line them up on a lightly floured board or tray in one layer and leave for 15 minutes to dry.

Prepare the mushroom and tomato sauce. Cook the ravioli in plenty of lightly salted, boiling water for 5 to 6 minutes or until they are just tender. Transfer to a heated serving bowl. Dot with butter and spoon over the mushroom and tomato sauce. Toss lightly and serve at once with the grated cheese on the side.

Liguria   **PANSÔTTI WITH**   Serves 4
WALNUT SAUCE
Pansôtti con salsa di noce

Pansôtti means pot bellied. These 'pot-bellied' ravioli are only found in Liguria where they are stuffed with *preboggion*, a mixture of wild herbs and greens. Pansôtti are always served with walnut sauce.

Filling
450g (1 lb) spinach
225g (8oz) borage or Swiss chard
1 bunch watercress
1 hard-boiled egg yolk
1 egg, beaten
100g (4oz) Ricotta cheese

40g (1½oz) freshly grated Parmesan cheese
¼ teaspoon freshly grated nutmeg
salt
freshly ground black pepper

Dough

300g (10oz) flour
3 eggs
½ teaspoon salt

Sauce

50g (2oz) shelled walnuts
2 tablespoons pine nuts, toasted in a 150°C (300°F/Gas
  Mark 2) oven until golden
1 garlic clove, crushed
1 small bunch parsley
75g (3oz) Ricotta cheese mixed with 3 tablespoons hot
  water
3 tablespoons olive oil
25g (1oz) butter
50g (2oz) freshly grated Parmesan cheese

Wash the spinach, borage and watercress and cook in a covered saucepan over a moderate heat for 5 minutes. The water clinging to the leaves is sufficient to prevent scorching. Drain, squeeze dry and chop.

Mash the egg yolk in a bowl and add the beaten egg, chopped greens, Ricotta cheese, Parmesan cheese, nutmeg and salt and black pepper to taste. Blend well together.

Follow the directions for egg pasta on page 98. Roll the dough out to two very thin sheets. Place teaspoonfuls of the filling over one sheet of the dough at regular intervals about 5cm (2 inches) apart. Cover with the other sheet of dough and press well around each mound. Cut the pansôtti into 5cm (2 inch) squares with a pastry or ravioli cutter. Line them up on a lightly floured board or tray in one layer and leave for 15 minutes to dry.

Meanwhile, prepare the sauce. Mix the walnuts, pine nuts, garlic, parsley and Ricotta cheese in a blender. Gradually add the olive oil to make a smooth sauce the consistency of soured cream. If the sauce is too thick, add a tablespoon or two of boiling water.

Cook the pansôtti in plenty of lightly salted, boiling water for 5 to 6 minutes or until they are just tender. Transfer to a heated serving bowl, dot with butter and spoon over the walnut sauce. Toss lightly and serve at once with the grated cheese on the side.

Lombardy **BUCKWHEAT NOODLES** Serves 6
WITH VEGETABLES
Pizzocheri

Pizzocheri is a speciality of the Valtellina Valley. The pasta dough is unique as it is made of a combination of buckwheat and wheat flour. It is cooked with a selection of vegetables, usually including potatoes, cabbage and green beans. The pasta and vegetables are layered with slices of the local Alpine cheese (Fontina makes an excellent substitute), sage and garlic-flavoured butter, and grated cheese. The dish is quickly baked in a hot oven until the cheese has melted.

Dough
225g (8oz) buckwheat flour
100g (4oz) strong white flour
2 eggs
2 tablespoons milk
½ teaspoon salt

Sauce
½ small Savoy cabbage
salt
3 medium potatoes
100g (4oz) French beans, cut into 5cm (2 inch) lengths
65g (2½oz) butter
3 garlic cloves, crushed
1 or 2 fresh sage leaves, chopped
100g (4oz) Fontina cheese, thinly sliced
75g (3oz) freshly grated Parmesan cheese

Combine the buckwheat and white flours in a bowl. Form a deep well in the centre and drop in 1 egg at a time followed by the milk and the salt. Gradually beat in the flour with a fork. Form into a soft ball, then knead for 8 to 10 minutes until the dough is smooth and elastic. If the dough is too soft, add a little extra flour. Do not add too much flour or the dough will be hard to handle.

Wrap the dough in a damp cloth and allow it to rest for 30 minutes. Roll out the dough as described on page 98, then cut into strips about 2.5 cm (1 inch) wide by 9 cm (3½ inches) long.

Cut the Savoy cabbage into pieces about 5 cm (2 inches) long by 2.5 cm (1 inch) wide. Bring 3.7 to 4 litres (7 to 8½ pints) of lightly salted water to the boil in a large saucepan. Add the potatoes, Savoy cabbage and French beans and cook for about 12 to 15 minutes or until almost tender. Add the buckwheat noodles and cook for a further 4 minutes or until the noodles are tender but still firm. Drain and return to the empty saucepan. Heat the butter in a small pan and sauté the garlic and sage for 2 minutes. Pour over the noodles and toss lightly.

Arrange a layer of the noodles and vegetables in a well-buttered shallow baking dish. Cover with slices of Fontina cheese and sprinkle with grated Parmesan. Repeat until the ingredients are used up. Top with Fontina cheese and grated Parmesan.

Place in a preheated oven at 200°C (400°F/Gas Mark 6) and bake for about 10 minutes or until the noodles are heated through and the cheese has melted. Serve at once with additional grated cheese on the side, if desired.

The vegetables in this recipe are usually cooked together with the pasta in a large saucepan of boiling water. If you prefer, you may steam the vegetables separately and combine them with the pasta after it has been cooked. This method prevents the vitamins from being lost in the cooking water.

Campania   **BAKED LASAGNE**   Serves 4 to 6
WITH AUBERGINE
Lasagna al forno

Dough
300g (10oz) flour
3 eggs
½ teaspoon salt

Filling
1 large aubergine (450–550g (1–1¼lb))
salt
120ml (4fl oz) olive oil
450ml (¾ pint) tomato sauce (see page 54)
225g (8oz) Mozzarella cheese, thinly sliced
450ml (¾ pint) béchamel sauce (see page 57)
100g (4oz) freshly grated Parmesan cheese

Peel the aubergine and cut it lengthwise into thin slices.
Sprinkle it with salt, set in a colander and leave to release
the bitter juices for 1 hour. Wash off the salt and pat the
slices dry with a paper towel.

Prepare the dough as in the recipe for egg pasta on page
98. Allow it to rest and then roll it out fairly thinly. Cut it
into rectangles about 11 × 18cm (4½ × 7 inches). Cook
about 6 lasagne at a time in plenty of lightly salted, boiling
water for 3 to 4 minutes. Remove with a slotted spoon and
dip into a bowl of cold water. Lay the lasagne flat on a
towel. Repeat until all the lasagne are cooked.

Heat the olive oil in a large frying pan and fry the
aubergine slices a few at a time, until golden on both sides.
Drain on a paper towel.

Grease a large shallow baking dish and arrange a layer
of lasagne over the bottom. Cover with fried aubergine,
spoon over a layer of tomato sauce and cover with slices of
Mozzarella cheese. Top with a thin layer of béchamel
sauce and sprinkle with grated Parmesan cheese. Repeat
until all the ingredients are used up, finishing with
lasagne, béchamel sauce and grated Parmesan cheese.
Bake in a preheated oven at 180°C (350°F/Gas Mark 4) for
30 to 40 minutes or until the top is golden.

Liguria and **GREEN LASAGNE** Serves 4
the North **WITH MUSHROOMS** to 6
Lasagne verde pasticciata con funghi

Dough
400g (14oz) flour
2 eggs
225g (8oz) spinach
½ teaspoon salt

Filling
350g (12oz) Ricotta cheese
450ml (¾ pint) mushroom and tomato sauce (see page 56)
450ml (¾ pint) béchamel sauce (see page 57)
100g (4oz) freshly grated Parmesan cheese

Prepare the dough as in the recipe for spinach pasta on page 99. Allow it to rest and then roll out fairly thinly. Cut into rectangles about 11 × 18 cm (4½ × 7 inches).

Cook about 6 lasagne at a time in plenty of lightly salted, boiling water for 3 to 4 minutes. Remove with a slotted spoon and dip into a bowl of cold water. Lay the lasagne flat on a towel. Repeat until all the lasagne are cooked.

Grease a large shallow baking dish and arrange a layer of lasagne over the bottom. Spoon a little Ricotta cheese over the bottom, cover with a little mushroom and tomato sauce, then béchamel sauce. Sprinkle some grated Parmesan over the top. Repeat the layers until all the ingredients are used up, finishing with lasagne, béchamel sauce and grated Parmesan cheese. Bake in a preheated oven at 180°C (350°F/Gas Mark 4) for 30 to 40 minutes or until the top is golden.

Piedmont	**BUTTERFLIES**	Serves 4
and the	**WITH THE**	to 6
North	**WHOLE GARDEN**	

Farfalle, tutto giardino

Farfalle are egg noodles made into the shape of butterflies.

25g (1oz) butter
2 tablespoons olive oil
2 garlic cloves, crushed
a handful of parsley, finely chopped
1 teaspoon fresh basil, or ¼ teaspoon dried
1 teaspoon fresh marjoram, or ¼ teaspoon dried
1 leek, thinly sliced
1 stalk celery, sliced
1 small courgette, sliced
175g (6oz) broccoli, broken into small florets
175g (6oz) French beans, cut into 2.5cm (1 inch) lengths
175g (6oz) fresh peas, shelled
100g (4oz) mushrooms, sliced
4 ripe plum tomatoes, peeled, seeded and chopped
120ml (4fl oz) vegetable stock
salt
freshly ground black pepper
350g (12oz) farfalle
100g (4oz) freshly grated Parmesan cheese

Heat 15g (½oz) butter and the olive oil in a large frying pan and cook the garlic, parsley, basil and marjoram for 1 minute. Add the leek, celery, courgette, broccoli, French beans and peas. Stir well and cook over a moderately high heat for 3 minutes. Add the mushrooms, tomatoes and stock, bring to the boil, cover and simmer for about 15 minutes or until the vegetables are just tender and the sauce is thickened. Season with salt and black pepper.

Cook the farfalle in plenty of lightly salted, boiling water. Drain and transfer to a heated serving bowl. Dot with the remaining butter and pour over the vegetable sauce. Toss lightly and serve at once with the grated cheese on the side.

Liguria   **EGG NOODLES WITH**   Serves 6
                    BEAN SAUCE
                  Fettucine al stufo

This is a speciality of La Spezia.

175g (6oz) dried white cannelini beans
2 tablespoons olive oil
2 garlic cloves, crushed
1 small onion, chopped
a pinch of rosemary
2 tablespoons fresh parsley, finely chopped
120ml (4fl oz) dry red wine
475ml (16fl oz) canned plum tomatoes, seeded and chopped
salt
freshly ground black pepper
675g (1½lb) egg noodles
25g (1oz) butter
100g (4oz) freshly grated Parmesan cheese

Soak the beans in water overnight and drain. Bring the beans to boil in 1.85 litres (3¼ pints) of water, cover and simmer for 1½ to 2 hours or until they are tender. Drain and set aside.

Heat the olive oil in a large frying pan and cook the garlic, onion, rosemary and parsley over a moderate heat for 3 minutes. Add the red wine and cook over a high heat until it has evaporated. Add the chopped tomatoes and continue to cook over a moderately high heat for 15 minutes or until the sauce starts to thicken. Add the drained beans and salt and black pepper to taste. Stir well and simmer for 5 minutes.

Cook the egg noodles in plenty of lightly salted, boiling water. Drain and transfer to a heated serving bowl. Dot with butter and pour over the hot sauce. Toss lightly and serve at once with the grated cheese on the side.

Calabria   **LINGUINE WITH**   Serves 6
                  BROCCOLI
                Linguine con broccoli

Variations of this dish are found from Calabria to Sicily. The broccoli is simmered in a rich tomato sauce flavoured with raisins, pine nuts and a dash of hot red pepper.

1 large head broccoli
2 tablespoons olive oil
1 garlic clove, crushed
1 small onion, chopped
¼ teaspoon hot red pepper flakes
120 ml (4 fl oz) dry red wine
475 ml (16 fl oz) canned plum tomatoes, seeded and chopped
40 g (1½ oz) pine nuts
40 g (1½ oz) raisins, soaked in hot water for 10 minutes
450 g (1 lb) linguine
100 g (4 oz) freshly grated Parmesan cheese

Break the broccoli into small florets and cut the stalks into bite-size pieces. Steam for about 10 minutes or until it is just tender.

Heat the olive oil in a large frying pan and cook the garlic, onion and hot pepper flakes over a moderate heat for 3 minutes. Add the wine and cook over a high heat until it has evaporated. Add the tomatoes and cook over a moderate heat for 20 to 25 minutes, or until the sauce starts to thicken. Add the pine nuts, raisins and cooked broccoli and simmer for 5 minutes.

Cook the linguine in plenty of lightly salted, boiling water. Drain and transfer to a heated serving bowl. Pour over the sauce, toss lightly and serve at once with grated cheese on the side.

Liguria   **TAGLIATELLE WITH**   Serves 4
              LEEKS
           Tagliatelle ai porri

This is a particularly light and delicious pasta sauce.

675g (1½lb) leeks
3 tablespoons olive oil
a handful of parsley, finely chopped
a pinch of rosemary
175g (6oz) canned plum tomatoes, forced through a sieve or
    puréed in a food processor
salt
freshly ground black pepper
450g (1lb) tagliatelle
25g (1oz) butter
100g (4oz) freshly grated Parmesan cheese

Trim away the roots of the leeks. Cut in half lengthwise
and carefully wash away the dirt that collects between the
leaves. Cut into slices 2.5cm (1 inch) long.

Heat the olive oil in a large frying pan and cook the
parsley and rosemary for 1 minute. Add the leeks and
cook gently for 10 minutes. Add the puréed tomatoes and
salt and black pepper to taste. Cover and simmer for 30
minutes.

Cook the tagliatelle in plenty of lightly salted, boiling
water. Drain and transfer to a heated serving bowl, dot
with butter and pour over the sauce. Toss lightly and serve
at once with the grated cheese on the side.

Emilia-   **EGG NOODLES WITH**   Serves 4
Romagna   **PEPPERS, PEAS AND**
                CREAM
           Fettucine ricche alla modenese

50g (2oz) butter
4 ripe plum tomatoes, peeled, seeded and chopped
175g (6oz) fresh shelled peas
2 red or yellow peppers

salt
freshly ground black pepper
450g (1 lb) egg noodles
120 ml (4 fl oz) double cream, brought just to the boil
100g (4 oz) freshly grated Parmesan cheese

Heat 25g (1oz) butter in a frying pan. Add the tomatoes and peas and cook over a moderate heat for 8 minutes.

Cook the peppers under a hot grill until the skin is blackened on both sides. Wash under cold water and remove the skins. Cut into small dice and add to the tomatoes and peas. Simmer for 5 minutes. Season with salt and black pepper to taste.

Cook the egg noodles in plenty of lightly salted, boiling water. Drain and transfer to a heated serving bowl. Dot with the remaining butter, pour over the hot cream and the vegetable sauce. Toss lightly and serve at once with the grated cheese on the side.

Apulia   **ORECCHIETTE WITH**   Serves 4
                 TURNIP TOPS
             Orecchiette con cime di rape

Orecchiette are short pasta shaped like 'little ears'. This dish is served without grated cheese.

50 ml (2 fl oz) olive oil
2 garlic cloves, crushed
⅛ teaspoon hot red pepper flakes
900g (2 lb) turnip tops, coarsely chopped
350g (12 oz) orecchiette

Heat the olive oil in a large frying pan and cook the garlic and hot pepper flakes for 1 minute. Add the turnip tops, cover and cook over a moderate heat for 7 to 8 minutes or until they are tender.

Cook the orecchiette in plenty of lightly salted, boiling water. Drain and transfer to a heated serving bowl. Cover with the turnip tops, toss lightly and serve at once.

Sicily

MACARONI WITH CAULIFLOWER, SULTANAS AND PINE NUTS
Maccheroni alla cappucina

Serves 4
to 5

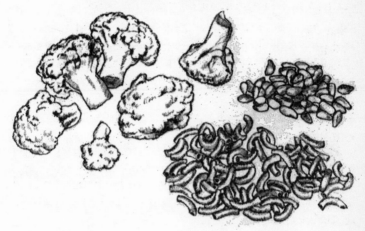

This is an unusual and exotic recipe.

350g (12oz) cauliflower, broken into small florets
2 tablespoons olive oil
1 small onion, chopped
½ teaspoon powdered saffron, dissolved in 50ml (2fl oz)
  boiling water
⅛ teaspoon ground cumin
40g (1½oz) pine nuts
40g (1½oz) sultanas, soaked for 10 minutes in hot water
350g (12oz) short macaroni
100g (4oz) freshly grated Pecorino cheese

Steam the cauliflower for 8 to 10 minutes or until just tender. Heat the olive oil in a large frying pan and gently cook the onion for 3 minutes. Add the cauliflower and cook over a moderate heat until golden. Add the saffron, cumin, pine nuts and sultanas and simmer for 5 minutes.

Cook the macaroni in plenty of lightly salted, boiling water. Drain and transfer to a heated serving bowl. Pour over the sauce. Toss lightly and serve at once with the grated cheese on the side.

Sicily   **VERMICELLI WITH**   Serves 4
AUBERGINE AND PEPPERS
Vermicelli alla siracusana

In this recipe from Syracuse in the south of Sicily, chopped aubergine and grilled peppers are simmered in a tomato sauce that is strongly flavoured with olives, capers and herbs. Caciocavallo cheese is often used in Sicily as a grating cheese instead of Pecorino or Parmesan cheese.

1 medium aubergine
2 yellow or green peppers
about 50ml (2fl oz) olive oil
2 garlic cloves, crushed
⅛ teaspoon hot red pepper flakes
225g (8oz) canned plum tomatoes, forced through a sieve or puréed in a food processor
12 Italian or Greek black olives, stoned and chopped
2 tablespoons capers
1 teaspoon fresh basil, or ¼ teaspoon dried
salt
450g (1lb) vermicelli
100g (4oz) freshly grated Caciocavallo cheese or Pecorino cheese

Trim the ends of the aubergine but do not peel it. Cut into 1 cm (½ inch) cubes. Cook the peppers under a hot grill until they are blackened all over. Rinse under cold water and remove the skins. Cut into 1 cm (½ inch) squares.

Heat the olive oil in a large frying pan and cook the garlic and hot pepper flakes for 1 minute. Add the aubergine and cook, covered, for 5 minutes until the aubergine is turning golden. Add the puréed tomatoes and cook over a moderate heat for 10 minutes. Add the diced peppers, olives, capers, basil, oregano and salt to taste and continue to cook for 5 minutes.

Cook the vermicelli in plenty of lightly salted, boiling water. Drain and transfer to a heated serving bowl. Pour over the aubergine sauce. Toss lightly and serve at once with the grated cheese on the side.

Sicily   **BUCATINI WITH**   Serves 4
**AUBERGINE, MUSHROOMS
AND MARSALA**
Bucatini con melanzane e funghi

1 medium aubergine (about 350g (12oz))
120ml (4fl oz) olive oil
1 small onion, finely chopped
25g (1oz) butter
1 garlic clove, crushed
a handful of parsley, finely chopped
1 tablespoon fresh basil, or ¼ teaspoon dried
225g (8oz) mushrooms, thinly sliced
50ml (2fl oz) dry Marsala
450g (1lb) bucatini
100g (4oz) freshly grated Parmesan cheese

Trim the ends of the aubergine, but do not peel it. Cut it into 1cm (½ inch) cubes. Heat the olive oil in a frying pan and cook the onion over a moderate heat for 3 minutes. Add the aubergine and cook over a moderate heat for 8 to 10 minutes, stirring often, until the aubergine is tender and turning golden.

Heat the butter in another frying pan and cook the garlic, parsley and basil for 1 minute. Add the mushrooms and cook over a moderate heat for 5 minutes. Add the Marsala and cook over a high heat until the liquid is almost evaporated and the mushrooms are tender. Mix the mushroom sauce with the fried aubergine and simmer together for 5 minutes.

Cook the bucatini in plenty of lightly salted, boiling water. Drain and transfer to a heated serving bowl. Pour over the sauce and serve at once with the grated cheese on the side.

Apulia   **FUSILLI WITH ROCKET**   Serves 4
Fusilli con la ruca

Fusilli are short pasta twisted like corkscrews. If rocket is not available, watercress may be used instead.

3 tablespoons olive oil
2 garlic cloves, crushed
1 small onion
475 ml (16 fl oz) canned plum tomatoes, seeded and chopped
salt
freshly ground black pepper
2 bunches rocket
450 g (1 lb) fusilli
100 g (4 oz) freshly grated Pecorino cheese

Heat the olive oil in a large frying pan and cook the garlic and onion over a moderate heat for 5 minutes until the onion is translucent. Add the tomatoes and cook over a high heat for 15 minutes or until the sauce is thickened. Season with salt and black pepper to taste. Wash the rocket and trim away the ends.

Cook the rocket with the fusilli in plenty of lightly salted, boiling water. Drain and transfer to a hot serving dish. Pour over the sauce, toss lightly and serve at once with the grated cheese on the side.

Sicily   **MACARONI AND**   Serves 4 to 6
              AUBERGINE PIE
              Pasta 'ncasciata

Sicilians like baked macaroni and vegetable pies. Although these are not as sophisticated as the lasagne of central Italy, they are particularly delicious and easy to prepare.

1 large aubergine (about 450 g (1 lb))
salt
120 ml (4 fl oz) olive oil
175 g (6 oz) fresh shelled peas
600 ml (1 pint) tomato sauce (see page 54)
350 g (12 oz) short macaroni (shells, ziti, penne, etc.)
2 hard-boiled eggs, sliced
175 g (6 oz) Caciocavallo or Mozzarella cheese
50 g (2 oz) freshly grated Pecorino cheese

Peel the aubergine and cut it into slices 5 mm (¼ inch) thick. Sprinkle with salt and set in a colander for 1 hour to release the bitter juices. Wash off the salt and pat dry. Fry the aubergine slices quickly in the hot oil until golden on both sides. Cook the peas in a little water for 12 to 15 minutes or until they are tender. Prepare the tomato sauce.

Cook the macaroni in plenty of lightly salted, boiling water. Drain and return to the saucepan. Pour over the tomato sauce and toss lightly.

Grease a large shallow baking dish and line the bottom with half the slices of fried aubergine. Cover with half the macaroni and tomato sauce. Arrange the slices of hard-boiled egg on top and scatter over the peas. Cover with slices of Caciocavallo or Mozzarella cheese and sprinkle with grated Pecorino cheese. Spread the rest of the fried aubergine over the top and cover with the remaining macaroni and sauce. Top with the remaining slices of Caciocavallo cheese and sprinkle with the remaining Pecorino cheese. Bake in a preheated oven at 180°C (350°F/Gas Mark 4) for 30 to 40 minutes or until the top is golden and the sauce is bubbling.

RICE
Il riso

Rice was first introduced to Italy by the Saracens. It is mainly grown in the north in the Po Valley which stretches from Piedmont through Lombardy to the Adriatic Sea.

In Italy, a risotto is always served as a separate course and never as a side dish. It is one of the most versatile dishes; almost any vegetable can be added to a risotto.

The cooking of risotto is unique. The rice is cooked in butter or oil and herbs for 1 minute, then a ladleful of hot stock is added. The rice is cooked over a moderately high heat in an open saucepan, while the cook watches and stirs, adding more hot stock as the liquid evaporates. The exact cooking time will depend on the age and absorbency of the rice. A little butter is stirred in at the end of cooking and additional grated cheese is served on the side.

Italian arborio rice is the best rice to use for risotto as it produces a creamy texture, while each grain is still *al dente*, or firm to the bite. Precooked or converted rice is unsuitable for risotto.

Lombardy   **SAFFRON RICE**   Serves 4
                  Risotto alla milanese

Saffron rice, or *risotto alla milanese*, could be called the national dish of Lombardy. Add the saffron towards the end of cooking to retain its delicate flavour. It is served as a separate course and is sometimes topped with mushrooms or truffles.

about 1 litre (1¾ pints) vegetable stock
25g (1oz) butter
1 small onion, finely chopped
300g (10oz) rice
½ teaspoon powdered saffron, or ½ teaspoon chopped
  whole saffron, soaked in 120ml (4fl oz) stock
75g (3oz) freshly grated Parmesan cheese
salt
freshly ground black pepper
1 truffle, sliced paper-thin (optional)
2 tablespoons double cream

Bring the stock to the boil in a pan and keep just below simmering point.

Heat the butter in a saucepan and cook the onion over a moderate heat for 5 minutes or until the onion is translucent. Stir in the rice and cook for 1 minute, so each grain is coated with butter. Add a ladleful of the stock. When the liquid has almost evaporated, add another ladleful of stock. Repeat until the rice is tender but still firm; this will take about 25 minutes. Five minutes before the end of cooking, add the saffron-flavoured stock, 25g (1oz) grated Parmesan cheese, salt and black pepper to taste and the truffle (if used). When the rice is cooked, stir in the double cream and serve at once with the remaining grated cheese on the side.

Lombardy   **RICE WITH LEEK**   Serves 4
            AND SWISS CHARD
            Ris porr e erbett

Sometimes served as soup.

about 1 litre (1¾ pints) vegetable stock or water
1 leek
2 tablespoons olive oil
a handful of parsley, finely chopped
450g (1 lb) Swiss chard, shredded
300g (10oz) rice
salt
freshly ground black pepper
25g (1oz) butter
100g (4oz) freshly grated Parmesan cheese

Bring the stock or water to the boil in a pan and keep just below simmering point.

Remove the root end of the leek and cut in half lengthwise. Wash away all the dirt that collects between the leaves and cut into thin slices (use the whole of the leek, including the dark green tops).

Heat the olive oil in a saucepan and add the parsley, leek and Swiss chard. Cook, covered, over a moderate heat for 10 minutes, stirring occasionally so the vegetables cook evenly. Stir in the rice and add a ladleful of stock. Cook until the liquid has almost evaporated. Add another ladleful of stock and repeat until the rice is tender but still firm. The finished risotto should be slightly creamy and the liquid should have evaporated. Season with salt and black pepper to taste. Stir in the butter and serve at once with the grated cheese on the side.

Tuscany **RICE WITH** Serves 4 to 6
SUMMER VEGETABLES
Risotto d'estate

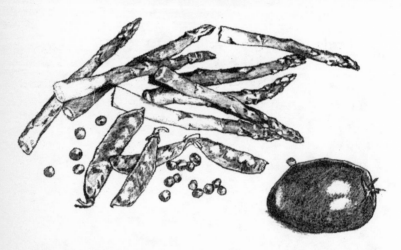

about 1 litre (1¾ pints) vegetable stock
100g (4oz) asparagus
3 tablespoons olive oil
1 small onion, chopped
1 tablespoon fresh basil, or ½ teaspoon dried
1 courgette, sliced
175g (6oz) fresh shelled peas
6 plum tomatoes, peeled, seeded and chopped
salt
freshly ground black pepper
300g (10oz) rice
½ teaspoon powdered saffron, or ½ teaspoon whole saffron,
    soaked in 120ml (4fl oz) of the stock
25g (1oz) butter
100g (4oz) freshly grated Parmesan cheese

Bring the stock to the boil in a saucepan and keep just
below simmering point.

Trim the ends of the asparagus and peel the stalks with
a sharp knife or vegetable peeler up to about 5cm (2
inches) from the tips. Cut diagonally into 2.5cm (1 inch)
lengths.

Heat the olive oil in a saucepan and cook the onion and basil over a moderate heat for 2 minutes. Add the courgette, asparagus, peas and 50 ml (2 fl oz) stock. Cover and simmer for 10 minutes. Add the chopped tomatoes with salt and black pepper to taste and simmer for a further 10 minutes. Add the rice and a ladleful of stock and cook until the liquid has almost evaporated. Add another ladleful of stock and repeat until the rice is tender but still firm. Five minutes before the end of cooking, add the saffron-flavoured stock and stir well. The finished risotto should be slightly creamy and the liquid should have evaporated. Stir in the butter and serve at once with the grated cheese on the side.

Veneto   **RICE WITH RAISINS**   Serves 4 to 6
AND PINE NUTS
Riso co'la ua

This is simple, exotic and delicious.

about 1.2 litres (2 pints) vegetable stock
2 tablespoons olive oil
1 garlic clove, crushed
1 small onion, finely chopped
a handful of parsley, finely chopped
120 ml (4 fl oz) dry white wine
350 g (12 oz) rice
75 g (3 oz) raisins
40 g (1½ oz) pine nuts
salt
freshly ground black pepper
25 g (1 oz) butter
75 g (3 oz) freshly grated Parmesan cheese

Bring the stock to the boil in a saucepan and keep just below simmering point.

Heat the olive oil in a saucepan and cook the garlic, onion and parsley over a moderate heat for 5 minutes or until the onion is translucent. Add the white wine and cook over a high heat until it has evaporated. Stir in the rice. Add a ladleful of stock and cook until the liquid has almost evaporated. Add another ladleful of stock, the raisins and pine nuts and repeat until the rice is tender but still firm. Season with salt and black pepper to taste. Stir in the butter and serve at once with the grated cheese on the side.

Lazio   **RICE WITH LENTILS**   Serves 6
Risotto con lenticche

Use small green lentils for this dish.

250g (9oz) green lentils
3 tablespoons olive oil
2 garlic cloves, crushed
1 small onion, chopped
1 stalk celery, thinly sliced
2 tablespoons parsley, finely chopped
225g (8oz) canned plum tomatoes, seeded and chopped
salt
freshly ground black pepper
250g (9oz) rice
25g (1oz) butter
75g (3oz) freshly grated Pecorino Romano cheese

Soak the lentils in water overnight and drain. Bring the lentils to the boil in about 1.2 litres (2 pints) water and simmer, covered, for 1½ hours or until they are tender. Do not drain.

Heat the olive oil in another saucepan and gently cook the garlic, onion, celery and parsley for 5 minutes. Add the chopped tomatoes and cook over a high heat for 10 minutes until the sauce is starting to thicken. Add the lentils and their cooking water (which should be about 750 ml (1¼ pints)) with salt and black pepper to taste.

Pour in the rice and simmer, covered, for 8 to 10 minutes or until the rice is tender but still firm and most of the liquid has evaporated. This risotto should not be too dry. Stir in the butter and serve at once with the grated cheese on the side.

Veneto   **RICE AND PEAS**   Serves 4
Risi e bisi

This is the most famous dish of the Veneto region. To retain the special quality of this dish fresh peas are a must. Choose the tiniest sweetest peas you can find.

about 1 litre (1¾ pints) vegetable stock or water
2 tablespoons olive oil
1 small onion, finely chopped
1 stalk celery, thinly sliced
2 tablespoons parsley, finely chopped
300g (10oz) rice
350g (12oz) young tender peas, shelled
salt
freshly ground black pepper
25g (1oz) butter
75g (3oz) freshly grated Parmesan cheese

Bring the stock to the boil in a saucepan and keep just below simmering point.

Heat the olive oil in a saucepan and cook the onion, celery and parsley over a moderate heat until they are turning golden.

Stir in the rice and cook for 1 minute, so each grain is coated with oil. Add a ladleful of stock and cook until the liquid is almost evaporated. Add another ladleful of stock and the peas with salt and black pepper to taste. Repeat until the rice is tender but still firm and the liquid has evaporated. Stir in the butter and serve at once with the grated cheese on the side.

Veneto   **RICE WITH FENNEL**   Serves 4
Risotto con fenoci

The Venetians like their risottos especially creamy. In Italian they say wavy or *ondosa*. Rice with fennel is particularly delicate and very delicious. Try it with a glass of chilled dry white wine, such as a Soave.

about 1 litre (1¾ pints) vegetable stock
1 large fennel bulb (about 350g (12oz))
2 tablespoons olive oil
1 small onion, chopped
300g (10oz) rice
salt
freshly ground black pepper
25g (1oz) butter
75g (3oz) freshly grated Parmesan cheese

Bring the stock to the boil in a saucepan and keep just below simmering point.

Trim away the stems and tough outer leaves of the fennel and cut the bulb into small dice.

Heat the olive oil in a saucepan and cook the onion and fennel over a moderate heat until they are starting to turn golden. Add the rice and cook for 1 minute, so each grain is coated with oil. Add a ladleful of stock, salt and black pepper to taste and cook until the liquid has almost evaporated. Add another ladleful of stock and repeat until the rice is tender but firm. Stir in the butter and serve at once with the grated cheese on the side.

Liguria   **RICE WITH COURGETTES**   Serves 4
                      AND PESTO
                 Risotto con zucchini e pesto

about 1 litre (1¾ pints) vegetable stock or water
3 small courgettes (about 350g (12oz))
3 tablespoons olive oil
2 garlic cloves, crushed
2 tablespoons parsley, finely chopped
300g (10oz) rice
25g (1oz) butter
3 tablespoons pesto sauce (see page 58)
50g (2oz) freshly grated Parmesan cheese

Bring the stock to the boil and keep just below simmering point.

Trim the ends of the courgettes and cut them into thin slices. Heat the olive oil in a saucepan and cook the garlic and parsley for 1 minute. Add the courgettes and cook over a moderately high heat until golden on both sides.

Add the rice and cook for 1 minute, so each grain is coated with oil. Add a ladleful of stock and cook until the liquid has almost evaporated. Repeat until the rice is tender but still firm and all the liquid has evaporated. Stir in the butter and pesto sauce and serve at once with the grated cheese on the side.

Lombardy   **ITALIAN FRIED RICE**   Serves 2 to 3
                Risotto al salto

This is more like a rice pancake than fried rice. Leftover risotto is combined with egg yolk and diced Mozzarella cheese and fried on both sides until crisp and golden.

300g (10oz) leftover saffron rice (see page 120)
1 egg yolk, beaten
40g (1½oz) Mozzarella cheese, cut into small dice
2 tablespoons olive oil
50g (2oz) freshly grated Parmesan cheese

Combine the leftover rice, egg yolk and Mozzarella cheese in a bowl. Mix lightly without mashing the rice.

Heat the olive oil in a frying pan and add the rice mixture. It should be about 1cm (½ inch) thick. Cook over a moderate heat for 5 to 6 minutes or until the bottom is golden. Place a saucepan lid or plate over the frying pan and quickly turn the pan over. Slide the rice back into the frying pan and cook until the rice is golden on the other side. Cut into wedges and serve with the grated cheese on the side.

Lombardy   **RICE WITH ONIONS**   Serves 3 to 4
La Risotta

This dish should be very liquid and creamy and is known
by the feminine nickname of *la Risotta.*

600 ml (1 pint) vegetable stock
40 g (1½ oz) butter
900 g (2 lb) onions
120 g (4½ oz) rice
½ teaspoon powdered saffron dissolved in 120 ml (4 fl oz)
    stock
salt
freshly ground black pepper
2 tablespoons double cream
75 g (3 oz) freshly grated Parmesan cheese

Bring the stock to the boil in a saucepan and keep just
below simmering point.

Heat the butter in a saucepan and cook the onions over
a moderate heat for 15 minutes or until they start to turn
light brown. Stir in the rice and cook for 1 minute, so each
grain is coated with butter. Add a ladleful of stock and
when the liquid is almost evaporated add another ladleful
of stock. Repeat until the rice is tender but still firm. This
will take about 25 minutes.

Five minutes before the end of cooking, add the saffron-
flavoured stock, salt and black pepper to taste. Do not let
the rice dry out; add a little more hot stock, if necessary.
When the rice is cooked, stir in the cream and serve at
once with the grated cheese on the side.

Piedmont   **SPINACH AND RICE PIE**   Serves 6
Turta

450 g (1 lb) fresh spinach
about 1 litre (1¾ pints) vegetable stock
2 tablespoons olive oil
1 small onion, finely chopped
a handful of parsley, finely chopped

1 teaspoon fresh marjoram, or ¼ teaspoon dried
300g (10oz) rice
50g (2oz) butter
5 eggs
100g (4oz) freshly grated Parmesan cheese
¼ teaspoon freshly grated nutmeg
salt
freshly ground black pepper

Wash the spinach and cook in a covered saucepan over a moderate heat for 5 minutes. The water clinging to the leaves is sufficient to prevent scorching. Drain, squeeze dry and chop, then set aside.

Bring the stock to the boil in a saucepan and keep just below simmering point.

Heat the olive oil in a saucepan and gently cook the onion, parsley and marjoram for 5 minutes or until the onion is translucent. Stir in the rice and cook for 1 minute, so each grain is coated with oil. Add a ladleful of stock and cook until the liquid has almost evaporated. Add another ladleful of stock and repeat until the rice is tender but still firm and all the liquid has evaporated.

Stir in 25g (1oz) butter, transfer the rice to a mixing bowl and allow it to cool slightly. Add the beaten eggs, chopped spinach, 50g (2oz) Parmesan cheese and nutmeg with salt and black pepper to taste. Mix together well. Pour into a well-buttered deep baking dish or soufflé dish and smooth the top with the back of a spoon.

Melt the remaining butter and dribble it over the top. Bake in a preheated oven at 190°C (375°F/Gas Mark 5) for 30 to 40 minutes or until the top is crisp and golden. Serve with the remaining grated cheese on the side.

POLENTA
Polenta

Polenta is a simple cornmeal mush that is one of the staple foods of Piedmont, Lombardy and the regions of the Veneto.

The name is derived from the Latin *pulmentum*, a mush made from finely ground grains that was passed on to the Romans by the Etruscans.

Polenta is usually made from cornmeal, but there is a version from the Valtellina Valley in Lombardy called *polenta taragna* that is made with buckwheat flour.

Polenta is traditionally made in a *paiolo* or unlined copper kettle and is always stirred with a wooden spoon or stick. Italian cornmeal, or *farina gialla*, comes in various degrees of fineness. I prefer the coarse variety found in Italian groceries, but finer cornmeal may be used instead.

The North
POLENTA
Polenta

about 1.6 litres (2¾ pints) water
1¼ teaspoons salt
about 255g (8oz) polenta

Bring the water to the boil in a large heavy saucepan. Add the salt and reduce the heat to simmer. Slowly pour in the polenta in a very thin stream, stirring constantly to prevent lumps from forming. Continue stirring for at least 45 minutes. If the polenta becomes too thick, add a little more boiling water. The polenta is cooked when it comes away from the sides of the pan and has lost any slight bitter taste.

The polenta may be eaten immediately with butter and cheese or the sauce of your choice, or it may be spread out on a work surface and left to harden. When cool, the polenta may be sliced like a cake and used as the foundation for various delicious pies or fritters.

Veneto
POLENTA AND CHEESE PIE
Polenta pastizzada

Serves 4 to 6

1 recipe polenta (see above)
225g (8oz) Fontina or Gruyère cheese, thinly sliced

450 ml (¾ pint) tomato sauce (see page 54)
100 g (4 oz) freshly grated Parmesan cheese

Prepare the polenta and spread it on a wooden board or baking sheet in a thin layer about 1 cm (½ inch) thick. Leave to cool. When cold, cut it into slices.

Butter a baking dish and arrange layers of polenta slices over the bottom. Cover with a layer of Fontina cheese, top with tomato sauce and sprinkle with grated Parmesan. Repeat the layers until all the ingredients are used up, finishing with tomato sauce and grated Parmesan. Bake in a preheated oven at 190°C (375°F/Gas Mark 5) for 20 minutes or until the top is golden and the sauce is bubbling.

Piedmont **POLENTA PIE** Serves 4
WITH MUSHROOMS to 6
Polenta pasticciata con funghi

1 recipe polenta (see page 130)
15 g (½ oz) butter
1 tablespoon olive oil
450 g (1 lb) mushrooms, thinly sliced
450 ml (¾ pint) béchamel sauce (see page 57)
50 g (2 oz) Gruyère cheese, grated
100 g (4 oz) freshly grated Parmesan cheese

Prepare the polenta and spread it on a wooden board or baking sheet in a thin layer 1 cm (½ inch) thick. Leave to cool. When cold, cut it into slices.

Heat the butter and olive oil in a frying pan and cook the mushrooms over a moderate heat for 5 minutes or until they are tender. Meanwhile, prepare the béchamel sauce. Remove from the heat and stir in the grated Gruyère cheese.

Butter a baking dish and arrange a layer of polenta slices over the bottom. Cover with a layer of mushrooms, spoon over the cheese sauce and sprinkle with grated Parmesan. Repeat the layers until all the ingredients are used up, finishing with the cheese sauce and grated cheese. Bake in a preheated oven at 190°C (375°F/Gas Mark 5) until the top is golden and the sauce is bubbling.

| Emilia-Romagna | **POLENTA AND BEANS** *Calzagatti* | Serves 4 to 6 |

This is a speciality of Modena.

175g (6oz) dried white haricot beans
salt
2 tablespoons olive oil
2 garlic cloves, crushed
1 small onion, finely chopped
225g (8oz) canned plum tomatoes, seeded and chopped
255g (8oz) polenta
50g (2oz) butter

Soak the beans in water overnight and drain. Bring the beans to the boil in unsalted boiling water and cook, covered, for 1½ hours or until they are tender. Season with salt, drain and reserve the cooking liquid.

Heat the olive oil in a frying pan and cook the garlic and onion over a moderate heat for 8-10 minutes or until the onion starts to turn golden. Add the tomatoes and cook over a high heat for 10 minutes until the sauce starts to thicken. Add to the drained beans and set aside.

Add sufficient water to the reserved cooking liquid to make 1.6 litres (2¾ pints) water. Bring to the boil in a heavy saucepan, add salt to taste and reduce the heat to a simmer. Slowly pour in the polenta in a very thin stream, stirring constantly to prevent lumps from forming. Continue stirring for at least 45 minutes. If the polenta becomes too thick, add a little more boiling water.

Just before the end of cooking remove the polenta from the heat and stir in the beans and tomato sauce and the butter. Return to the heat and cook for a further 5 minutes, stirring constantly. Serve at once.

Calzagatti may also be cooled, cut into squares and deep fried in hot oil until golden and crisp.

Piedmont   **FRIED POLENTA**   Serves 4 to 6
                    SANDWICHES
                 Polenta in carozza

1 recipe polenta (see page 130)
225 g (8 oz) Fontina cheese
flour for dusting
2 eggs, beaten
dry breadcrumbs
oil for frying

Prepare the polenta and spread it on a wooden board or baking sheet in a thin layer about 1 cm (½ inch) thick. Cut into 7.5 cm (3 inch) rounds with a glass or a biscuit cutter. Cut the Fontina cheese into rounds the same size as the polenta and sandwich each cheese slice between rounds of polenta. Press well together so the filling will not fall out.

Dip the sandwiches in flour, then beaten egg, then breadcrumbs and fry in hot oil until golden on both sides. Drain on a paper towel and serve at once.

DUMPLINGS
Gnocchi

Most regions of Italy have their own versions of gnocchi. They are usually made with mashed potatoes or semolina flour, or a mixture of spinach and Ricotta cheese. In Liguria gnocchi are sometimes made with chestnut flour and served with walnut sauce. 'Gnocchi di zucca', a speciality of Lombardy, are made with mashed pumpkin, egg, flour, cinnamon and crushed macaroons.

Gnocchi, like pasta, are cooked in plenty of lightly salted, boiling water. Just before they are cooked they float to the surface where they can be easily removed with a slotted spoon and the next batch put on to cook.

Gnocchi may be served simply with butter and cheese, or with the sauce of your choice.

Campania   **POTATO DUMPLINGS**   Serves 6
Strangugli or *Strangulaprieviti*

This version of potato dumplings is made without eggs. The exact amount of flour needed will depend upon the moisture content of the potatoes; too much flour will make the dumplings tough and heavy. To test, try putting one dumpling in boiling water to be sure that it holds its shape without falling apart.

900g (2lb) old potatoes
about 200g (7oz) wholemeal or plain white flour
1 teaspoon salt
450ml (¾ pint) tomato sauce (see page 54)
100g (4oz) freshly grated Pecorino cheese

Boil the potatoes in lightly salted water for 20 minutes or until they are tender. Drain and remove the skins when they are cool enough to handle. Force through a sieve and allow to drop on a lightly floured board or work surface. While the potatoes are still warm, work in the flour and salt to make a soft dough. Roll the dough into long cylinders about the thickness of your finger, then cut into 2.5 cm (1 inch) lengths. Press each piece with your index finger against the inside of a fork, forming a crescent shape with an indent on the inside where your finger was and ridges on the outside from the fork.

Drop about half of the gnocchi into a large saucepan of lightly salted, boiling water. The gnocchi will float to the surface just before they are cooked. Cook for 1-2 minutes longer, then remove with a slotted spoon and transfer to a heated serving bowl. Spoon over a little hot tomato sauce. Repeat with the remaining gnocchi. Cover with the remaining sauce and serve at once with the grated cheese on the side.

Lazio   **BAKED SEMOLINA**   Serves 4
GNOCCHI
Gnocchi alla romana

450 ml (¾ pint) milk
450 ml (¾ pint) water
150 g (5 oz) semolina
100 g (4 oz) butter, softened
⅛ teaspoon freshly grated nutmeg
salt
freshly ground black pepper
2 egg yolks
150 g (5 oz) freshly grated Parmesan cheese

Bring the milk and water to the boil in a saucepan over a moderate heat. Slowly pour in the semolina in a thin stream, stirring constantly. Add 25 g (1 oz) butter, nutmeg, salt and black pepper to taste and cook for a further 15 minutes, stirring frequently. Remove from the heat and add the egg yolks and 25g (1oz) of the grated cheese. Blend well together.

Moisten a baking sheet with cold water and pour on the semolina mixture. Spread it out evenly with a wet spatula into a layer about 5mm (¼ inch) thick. Allow to cool for 1 hour or until the semolina is quite firm. Cut out 4cm (1½ inch) rounds with a biscuit cutter or a small glass.

Arrange 2 or 3 layers of gnocchi rounds in a well-buttered baking dish. Sprinkle each layer with Parmesan cheese and dot with the remaining butter. Bake in a preheated oven at 190°C (375°F/Gas Mark 5) for 15 to 20 minutes or until the gnocchi are golden.

Tuscany	**SWISS CHARD AND**	Serves 4
	RICOTTA DUMPLINGS	

Strozzapreti alla fiorentina

Strozzapreti, like the Neapolitan *strangulaprievete*, means 'priest-strangler'. The name probably alludes to the clergy's reputed gluttony – the priests were said to eat these dumplings so quickly that they would choke on them. Most recipes for *strozzapreti* include a little flour in the dumpling mixture, but I find that if you squeeze most of the moisture out of the cooked Swiss chard, no flour is necessary. Simply dipping the gnocchi into flour before cooking is sufficient to hold them together. The cooking time is very quick – about 3 minutes.

900g (2lb) Swiss chard
350g (12oz) Ricotta cheese
2 egg yolks
75g (3oz) freshly grated Parmesan cheese
¼ teaspoon freshly grated nutmeg
⅛ teaspoon cinnamon
salt
freshly ground black pepper
flour
50g (2oz) butter

Cook the Swiss chard in a covered saucepan over a moderate heat for 5 minutes. The water clinging to the leaves is sufficient to prevent scorching. Drain, squeeze dry and chop coarsely. Place the chard in a mixing bowl with the Ricotta cheese, egg yolks, 40g (1½oz) Parmesan cheese, nutmeg, cinnamon and salt and black pepper to taste. Blend well together. Cover the bowl and refrigerate for 2 hours.

Form the mixture into long sausage shapes about 2cm (¾ inch) in diameter and cut into 2.5cm (1 inch) lengths. Dip the gnocchi lightly in flour and drop about half of the dumplings into rapidly boiling, lightly salted water. The dumplings will float to the surface when they are cooked. Remove with a slotted spoon and transfer to a hot serving bowl. Dot with half the butter and sprinkle with half of the remaining grated cheese. Repeat with the remaining dumplings and top with the remaining butter and grated cheese.

MAIN COURSES

PIES AND TARTS
Torte e Crostate

Pies and tarts make excellent lunch or supper dishes, served with a salad and followed by dessert. They are usually made of unsweetened shortcrust pastry or a paper-thin strudel-type pastry. Pies may be filled with vegetables in cream sauces, cheese and vegetable custards, and some stews or gratins.

The pies and tarts in this chapter are made with short-crust pastry or filo pastry, which makes an excellent substitute for strudel pastry.

If you are using frozen filo pastry, thaw it for a minimum of 2 hours before using so each sheet can be easily separated. If two sheets stick together, use them as if they were one. Simply brush them with oil and continue.

Work as quickly as possible, as filo pastry hardens very quickly. Keep the sheets of pastry covered with a clean damp cloth as you prepare them to prevent them drying out.

SHORTCRUST PASTRY
Pasta frolla

Makes enough for a 23 or 25 cm (9 or 10 inch) flan case

A good shortcrust pastry is crisp and buttery when baked. Work very quickly while you make this pastry. If the dough is worked too much, it becomes hard to handle. Wholemeal or plain white flour or a combination of both may be used.

225 g (8 oz) wholemeal or plain white flour
¼ teaspoon salt
100 g (4 oz) chilled butter, cut into very small cubes
about 4 tablespoons water

Sift the flour and salt into a mixing bowl. Add the butter. Rub the butter into the flour with your fingertips until the mixture resembles coarse breadcrumbs. Working very quickly, sprinkle on enough iced water to form into a soft ball. The dough should not be sticky. Wrap in foil and refrigerate for 30 minutes before rolling out.

Place the dough on a lightly floured board and knead it briefly. Roll out into a circle about 30 cm (12 inches) in diameter and 3 mm (⅛ inch) thick. (Any extra dough can be used for tartlets.) Carefully roll the dough around the rolling pin and unroll it on to a well-buttered flan tin. Trim away any excess dough and flute the edges with a fork. Prick the bottom in a few places. Cover the dough with a sheet of foil and fill with dried beans; this prevents the flan case from puffing up while baking.

For a partially baked flan case, preheat the oven to 200°C (400°F/Gas Mark 6) and bake the pastry for 8 to 10 minutes. The pastry should have shrunk away slightly from the sides of the tin. Remove from the oven and carefully remove the foil and dried beans.

For a fully baked flan case, return to the oven. Prick the bottom again and bake for another 8 to 10 minutes until the pastry is very light brown.

Liguria   **EASTER PIE**   Serves 6
La torta pasqualina

La torta pasqualina is a famous Genoese speciality. It is made of layers of paper-thin pastry filled with Swiss chard and a Ricotta-type cheese called *quagliata*. Depressions are made in the cheese at regular intervals and an egg is broken into each. More layers of pastry are spread on top and the whole thing is baked in the oven. Frozen filo pastry, available in many delicatessens and supermarkets, makes this elaborate pie very easy to prepare. The accomplished cook who wants to prepare the pastry at home should note that it is not possible to make the pastry sheets as thin as commercial filo pastry, so fewer sheets are required.

Pastry
450g (1 lb) plain white flour
½ teaspoon salt
about 175 ml (6 fl oz) water
1 tablespoon olive oil

Filling
900g (2 lb) Swiss chard or spinach
about 120 ml (4 fl oz) olive oil
1 teaspoon fresh marjoram, or ½ teaspoon dried
75g (3 oz) freshly grated Parmesan cheese
350g (12 oz) Ricotta cheese
50 ml (2 fl oz) double cream
1 tablespoon plain white flour
¼ teaspoon ground cinnamon
¼ teaspoon freshly grated nutmeg
salt
freshly grated black pepper

6 eggs
25g (1oz) butter, melted

To make the pastry, place the flour and salt in a mixing bowl. Make a well in the centre and add the water and olive oil. Work into a soft dough. Knead well for about 15 minutes until the dough is smooth and elastic, adding a little more water if necessary. The exact quantity of water depends upon the absorbency of the flour. Wrap the dough in a damp cloth and let it rest for 1 hour.

To make the filling, wash the Swiss chard and cook it in a covered saucepan over a moderate heat for 5 minutes. Drain, squeeze dry and chop coarsely. Heat 2 tablespoons olive oil in a saucepan, add the marjoram and Swiss chard and cook gently for 5 minutes. Remove from the heat and stir in 25g (1oz) Parmesan cheese. Set aside.

In a bowl, combine the Ricotta cheese, cream, flour, cinnamon and nutmeg with salt and black pepper to taste. Blend well.

Divide the dough into 10 equal portions and roll out each portion on a lightly floured board. Knead them briefly and roll out as thinly as possible. Stretch each piece of dough out with the hands into rectangles about 33 × 23 cm (13 × 9 inches).

Place a sheet of pastry (or filo pastry if used) over the bottom of a well-greased baking tin about 28 × 18 cm (11 × 7 inches) and at least 5 cm (2 inches) deep. Brush the top with olive oil and place another sheet of pastry on top. Repeat until 6 sheets of pastry are used (10 sheets if using filo pastry). Spread the Swiss chard evenly over the pastry and cover with the Ricotta cheese mixture. With the back of a spoon, make indentations over the filling deep enough to hold an egg. Break 1 egg into each hollow and sprinkle the top lightly with salt, black pepper and the remaining grated cheese. Dribble the melted butter over the top.

Very carefully place a sheet of pastry or filo pastry over the top; do not press it down. Brush lightly with olive oil and repeat with the remaining sheets of pastry. Use as light a hand as possible. Bake in a preheated oven at 160°C (325°F/Gas Mark 3) for about 1 hour.

Liguria	**SPINACH PIE**	Serves 6
	La torta d'erbette	

This is a simpler version of the Easter Pie.

900g (2lb) fresh spinach, beet leaves or Swiss chard
25g (1oz) butter
1 leek, thinly sliced
a handful of parsley, chopped
350g (12oz) Ricotta cheese
3 eggs
100g (4oz) freshly grated Parmesan cheese
⅛ teaspoon freshly grated nutmeg
salt
freshly ground black pepper
1 recipe pastry (as for Easter Pie – see page 140), or 15
  sheets thawed filo pastry
about 120ml (4floz) olive oil

Wash the spinach carefully and cook in a covered saucepan over a moderate heat for 5 minutes. Drain, squeeze dry and chop it coarsely.

Heat the butter in a large frying pan and cook the leek and parsley over a moderate heat for 8 to 10 minutes or until the leek is tender. Add the chopped spinach and cook for 1 minute.

Mix the Ricotta cheese, eggs and Parmesan cheese in a large bowl. Add the nutmeg, salt and black pepper to taste and blend well. Place a sheet of pastry or filo pastry over the bottom of a well-greased baking tin about 5cm (2 inches) deep. Brush the top with olive oil and place another sheet of pastry on top. Repeat until 6 sheets of pastry (or 10 sheets of filo pastry) are used up.

Combine the cooked spinach mixture with the cheese mixture and spread over the pastry. Place a sheet of pastry or filo pastry on top and brush lightly with olive oil. Repeat with the remaining sheets of pastry. Bake in a preheated oven at 180°C (350°F/Gas Mark 4) for 30 to 40 minutes or until the top is golden and the pie is puffed up.

Liguria **MUSHROOM AND COURGETTE PIE** Serves 6 to 8
La torta di funghi e zucchini

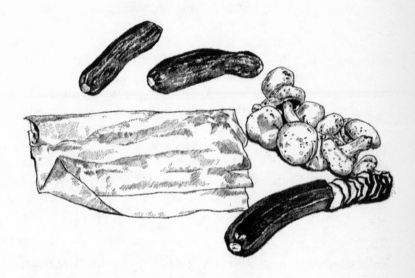

Another delicious vegetable pie from Liguria.

25 g (1 oz) butter
2 tablespoons fresh parsley, finely chopped
450 g (1 lb) mushrooms, thinly sliced
about 175 ml (6 fl oz) olive oil
4 small courgettes (about 450–550 g (1¼ lb)), thinly sliced
350 g (12 oz) Ricotta cheese
3 eggs
50 g (2 oz) freshly grated Parmesan cheese
⅛ teaspoon freshly grated nutmeg
salt
freshly ground black pepper
1 recipe pastry (as for Easter Pie – see page 140) or 15
*   sheets thawed filo pastry*

Heat the butter in a large frying pan and cook the parsley for 1 minute. Add the mushrooms and cook over a moderate heat for 5 minutes or until just tender. Set aside.

Heat 3 tablespoons of the olive oil in another large frying pan and cook the courgettes over a moderately high heat until golden on both sides. Set aside.

Mix the Ricotta cheese, eggs and Parmesan cheese in a large bowl. Add the nutmeg and salt and black pepper to taste.

Place a sheet of pastry or filo pastry over the bottom of a well-greased baking tin about 5cm (2 inches) deep. Brush the top with olive oil and place another sheet of pastry on top. Repeat until 6 sheets of pastry (or 10 sheets of filo pastry) are used up. Cover with the fried courgette slices. Spread over the Ricotta cheese mixture and top with the fried mushrooms. Place a sheet of pastry or filo pastry over the top and brush lightly with olive oil. Repeat with the remaining sheets of pastry. Bake in a preheated oven at 180°C (350°F/Gas Mark 4) for 30 to 40 minutes, or until the top is golden and the flan is puffed up.

Valle d'Aosta   **ONION TART**   Serves 4 to 6
                        Crostata di cipolle

This is one of my favourite tarts. The onion should be cooked very slowly, without browning, until they are almost reduced to a purée, then add the eggs and cream.

900g (2lb) onions
2 tablespoons olive oil
15g (½oz) butter
250ml (8floz) double cream
2 eggs
25g (1oz) freshly grated Parmesan cheese
⅛ teaspoon freshly grated nutmeg
salt
freshly ground black pepper
a 23cm (9 inch) partially baked flan case (see page 139)

Peel the onions and slice them very thinly. Heat the olive oil and butter in a large frying pan and add the onions. Cover and cook gently for 25 to 30 minutes or until they are very soft. Do not allow to brown.

Beat the cream and eggs together in a bowl. Add the onions, Parmesan cheese, nutmeg and salt and pepper to taste. Pour into the partially baked flan case and bake in a preheated oven at 190°C (375°F/Gas Mark 5) for 30 minutes or until the tart is lightly browned and puffed up.

Emilia-Romagna | **MUSHROOM TART** | Serves 4 to 6
Crostata di funghi

40g (1½oz) butter
1 small onion, chopped
2 tablespoons parsley, finely chopped
1 teaspoon fresh marjoram, or ¼ teaspoon dried
450g (1lb) fresh mushrooms, thinly sliced
3 tablespoons dry Marsala
3 eggs
350ml (12floz) double cream
salt
freshly ground black pepper
a 23cm (9 inch) partially baked flan case (see page 139)

Heat the butter in a large frying pan and cook the onion, parsley and marjoram for 1 minute. Add the mushrooms and cook for 5 minutes. Add the Marsala, increase the heat and cook until the liquid has evaporated.

Beat the eggs and cream together in a bowl. Stir in the mushroom mixture and season with salt and black pepper to taste. Pour into the partially baked flan case and bake in the centre of a preheated oven at 190°C (375°F/Gas Mark 5) for 30 minutes or until the tart is lightly browned and puffed up.

Lombardy and the North | **PEA AND LETTUCE TART** | Serves 4 to 6
Crostata di piselli e lattugha

450g (1lb) shelled peas
1 tablespoon olive oil

25g (1oz) butter
1 Webb's lettuce, shredded
a handful of fresh parsley, chopped
3 eggs
250 ml (8fl oz) double cream
120ml (4fl oz) milk
40g (1½) freshly grated Parmesan cheese
salt
freshly ground black pepper
a 23cm (9 inch) partially baked flan case (see page 139)

Cook the peas in lightly salted boiling water for 10 to 30 minutes until they are tender. The exact cooking time depends on their age and size.

Heat the olive oil and butter in a large frying pan. Add the lettuce and parsley and cook, covered, over a moderate heat for 5 minutes or until the lettuce has wilted. Increase the heat, if necessary, to evaporate any excess moisture. Add the cooked peas, stir well and cook for 1 minute.

Beat the eggs, cream and milk together in a bowl. Add the pea mixture, Parmesan cheese and salt and black pepper to taste. Blend well. Pour into the partially baked flan case and bake in the centre of a preheated oven at 190°C (375°F/Gas Mark 5) for 30 minutes or until the tart is lightly browned and puffed up.

Emilia-Romagna **ASPARAGUS TART** Serves 4 to 6
Crostata di asparagii

450g (1lb) asparagus
3 eggs
250ml (8fl oz) double cream
120ml (4fl oz) milk
50g (2oz) freshly grated Parmesan cheese
⅛ teaspoon freshly grated nutmeg
salt
freshly ground black pepper
a 23cm (9 inch) partially baked flan case (see page 139)

Trim the tough ends of the asparagus and peel the stalks with a sharp knife or vegetable peeler up to about 5 cm (2 inches) from the tips. Steam for 20 minutes or until the asparagus is tender. Cut diagonally into 2.5 cm (1 inch) lengths.

In a bowl beat the eggs, cream, milk, Parmesan cheese and nutmeg with salt and black pepper. Lightly stir in the cooked asparagus. Pour into the partially baked flan case and bake in the centre of a preheated oven at 190°C (375°F/Gas Mark 5) for 30 minutes or until the tart is lightly browned and puffed up.

| Lombardy | **LEEK TART** | Serves 4 to 6 |
| | *Crostata di porri* | |

450 g (1 lb) leeks
2 tablespoons olive oil
25 g (1 oz) butter
2 tablespoons flour
300 ml (10 fl oz) milk
75 g (3 oz) grated Gruyère cheese
2 eggs, beaten
salt
freshly ground black pepper
a 23 cm (9 inch) partially baked flan case (see page 139)

Trim the root ends of the leeks. Cut in half lengthwise and wash away the dirt that collects between the leaves. Cut into 2.5 cm (1 inch) lengths. Heat the olive oil in a saucepan, add the leeks, cover and cook gently for 20 minutes or until the leeks are very soft.

Prepare a béchamel sauce using the butter, flour and milk (for instructions, see page 57). Remove from the heat and stir in the Gruyère cheese, the eggs and the leeks. Season with salt and black pepper.

Pour the mixture into the partially baked flan case and bake in the centre of a preheated oven at 190°C (375°F/Gas Mark 5) for 30 minutes or until the tart is lightly browned and puffed up.

Liguria   **SWISS CHARD TART**   Serves 4 to 6
             Crostata di bietole

Swiss chard and spinach tarts are made all over northern
Italy. This version tastes particularly good, although the
addition of currants may seem rather unusual.

900g (2lb) Swiss chard
2 tablespoons olive oil
25g (1oz) grated Fontina cheese
1 egg
2 tablespoons currants
⅛ teaspoon freshly grated nutmeg
salt
freshly ground black pepper
a 23cm (9 inch) partially baked flan case (see page 139)

Wash the Swiss chard and cook in a covered saucepan over
a moderate heat for 5 minutes until tender. The water
clinging to the leaves is sufficient to prevent scorching.
Drain, squeeze dry and chop coarsely.

Heat the olive oil in a pan and cook the chopped Swiss
chard for 2 minutes. Place in a bowl and add the Fontina
cheese, egg, currants and nutmeg with salt and black
pepper to taste. Blend well together.

Pour the mixture into the partially baked flan case and
bake in the centre of a preheated oven at 190°C (375°F/Gas
Mark 5) for 25 minutes.

GRATINS AND CASSEROLES
Timballi, Tortini, Polpettone, etc.

A gratin is literally the crust that is formed when a dish is
browned in the oven or under a grill. The gratins in this
chapter consist of vegetables or combinations of
vegetables, with or without a sauce, that are topped with
breadcrumbs or grated cheese and baked in the oven.

A casserole is a one-dish meal that can be made in
advance. It usually includes pasta or rice, vegetables and a

sauce, and is baked in the oven.

Both gratins and casseroles may be prepared ahead of time and baked in the oven at the last minute. They make delicious and unusual main courses.

Abruzzi **AUBERGINE TIMBALE** Serves 4
Timballo di melanzane

Scamorza is a fresh cheese made in the Abruzzi and Campania that is good for cooking. Mozzarella makes an excellent substitute.

2 aubergines (about 675 g (1½ lb))
salt
flour
about 120 ml (4 fl oz) olive oil
175 g (6 oz) Scamorza or Mozzarella cheese, thinly sliced
2 eggs, beaten
freshly ground black pepper
25 g (1 oz) freshly grated Pecorino cheese

Trim the ends of the aubergines, but do not peel them. Cut into slices 3 mm (⅛ inch) thick, sprinkle with salt and set in a colander for 1 hour to release the bitter juices. Wash off the salt and pat the slices dry with a paper towel. Dip in flour and quickly fry in hot olive oil until golden on both sides. Drain on a paper towel.

Arrange a layer of fried aubergine on the bottom of a shallow baking dish. Cover with slices of Scamorza cheese, a little beaten egg and sprinkle with salt and black pepper. Repeat the layers until all the ingredients are used up. Sprinkle the top with grated Pecorino cheese and bake in a preheated oven at 180°C (350°F/Gas Mark 4) for 30 minutes or until the top is golden.

Campania **COURGETTE PARMIGIANA**   Serves 4
Zucchini alla parmigiana

5 or 6 courgettes (about 675g (1½lb))
flour
about 120ml (4floz) olive oil
450ml (¾ pint) tomato sauce (see page 54)
225g (8oz) Mozzarella cheese, thinly sliced
100g (4oz) freshly grated Parmesan cheese

Trim the courgettes and cut them lengthwise into slices about 3mm (⅛ inch) thick. Dip in flour and fry in hot olive oil until golden on both sides. Drain on a paper towel.

Arrange a layer of fried courgettes on the bottom of a shallow baking dish. Cover with some tomato sauce, top with slices of Mozzarella cheese and sprinkle with grated Parmesan. Repeat the layers until all the ingredients are used up, finishing with Mozzarella and Parmesan cheese. Bake in a preheated oven at 190°C (375°F/Gas Mark 5) for 25 to 30 minutes or until the top is golden and the sauce is bubbling.

Campania **AUBERGINE, COURGETTE**   Serves 4
AND POTATO PIE   to 6
Tortino di verdure

Vegetable and cheese casseroles are common all over Italy. This version from the region around Naples is a particularly satisfying and delicious combination.

1 small aubergine (about 225g (8oz))
salt
2 medium potatoes, peeled
2 small courgettes
about 120ml (4floz) olive oil
1 large onion, peeled and thinly sliced
freshly ground black pepper
225g (8oz) Mozzarella cheese, thinly sliced
3 eggs, beaten
25g (1oz) wholemeal breadcrumbs
15g (½oz) fresh parsley, finely chopped

Peel the aubergine and cut it into slices 5mm ($\frac{1}{4}$ inch) thick. Sprinkle with salt and set in a colander for 1 hour to release the bitter juices. Wash off the salt and pat dry with a paper towel.

Boil the potatoes in lightly salted water for 20 minutes or until they are tender. Drain, cool and cut into slices 3mm ($\frac{1}{8}$ inch) thick.

Trim the courgettes and cut them lengthwise into thin slices. Heat 50ml (2floz) olive oil in a large frying pan and quickly fry the aubergine on both sides until golden. Drain on a paper towel. Add a tablespoon or two of oil to the same frying pan and quickly fry the courgettes on both sides until golden. Drain on a paper towel. Add a further 2 tablespoons of oil and cook the onion over a moderate heat for 7 minutes or until translucent.

Arrange the potatoes in the bottom of a well-greased baking dish. Top with a few slices of Mozzarella cheese and a little beaten egg. Sprinkle lightly with breadcrumbs and a few drops of the remaining olive oil. Cover with aubergine slices, Mozzarella cheese, breadcrumbs, beaten egg and olive oil. Repeat the layers using courgettes instead of the aubergines. Cover with the onions and top with the remaining Mozzarella cheese, beaten egg and breadcrumbs. Season with some black pepper and dribble over 1 or 2 tablespoons of olive oil. Bake in a preheated oven at 180°C (350°F/Gas Mark 4) for 30 to 40 minutes or until the top is golden. Serve sprinkled with chopped parsley.

Liguria   **GREEN BEAN AND**   Serves 4 to 6
                   POTATO PUDDING
                   Polpettone di fagiolini e patate

Elsewhere in Italy *polpettone* means a croquette. In Liguria, *polpettone* is a vegetable purée mixed with eggs and sometimes Ricotta cheese and baked in a crust of butter and breadcrumbs.

450g (1lb) French beans
450g (1lb) potatoes
salt
4 eggs
50g (2oz) freshly grated Parmesan cheese
2 tablespoons olive oil
2 garlic cloves, crushed
2 tablespoons fresh parsley, finely chopped
2 teaspoons fresh marjoram, or ½ teaspoon dried
freshly ground black pepper
25g (1oz) wholemeal breadcrumbs
25g (1oz) butter

Top and tail the beans and steam them for 15 minutes or until tender. Peel the potatoes and boil in lightly salted water for 20 minutes or until they are tender. Force the beans and potatoes through a sieve or purée in a blender with a little liquid from the boiled potatoes. Blend in the eggs, one at a time, and stir in the Parmesan cheese.

Heat the olive oil in a small frying pan and cook the garlic, parsley and marjoram for 1 minute. Add the bean mixture, season with salt and black pepper and mix well.

Grease the bottom and sides of a large, shallow baking dish. Dust with half the breadcrumbs, turn the baking dish over and shake out any excess crumbs. Pour in the bean mixture, top with the remaining breadcrumbs and dot with butter. Bake in a preheated oven at 180°C (350°F/Gas Mark 4) for 45 to 50 minutes or until it is nicely puffed up and the top is golden.

Liguria   **POTATO, SPINACH AND**   Serves 4
               PEA PUDDING   to 6
        Polpettone di patate, spinaci e piselli

This is sometimes called *la torta verde* or 'green pie'.

250g (9oz) fresh shelled peas
900g (2lb) potatoes
225g (8oz) spinach
4 eggs, beaten well
75g (3oz) freshly grated Parmesan cheese
100g (4oz) Mozzarella cheese, thinly sliced
salt
freshly ground black pepper
25g (1oz) wholemeal breadcrumbs
25g (1oz) butter

Boil the peas for 15 to 30 minutes until tender. The exact time will depend upon the age and size of the peas. Force through a sieve or purée in a blender and set aside.

Peel the potatoes and boil in lightly salted water for 20 minutes or until they are tender. Force through a sieve and set aside.

Wash the spinach carefully and cook in a covered saucepan over a moderate heat for 5 minutes. The water clinging to the leaves is sufficient to prevent scorching. Drain, squeeze dry, chop coarsely and purée in a blender. Combine the pea, potato and spinach purées in a large bowl. Stir in the beaten eggs and grated Parmesan and season to taste with salt and black pepper.

Grease the bottom and sides of a large, shallow baking dish and sprinkle with half the breadcrumbs. Turn the baking dish over and shake out any excess crumbs. Pour in half the potato mixture. Cover with slices of Mozzarella cheese. Pour over the remaining potato mixture, sprinkle with the remaining breadcrumbs and dot with butter. Bake in a preheated oven at 180°C (350°F/Gas Mark 4) for 45 to 50 minutes or until the pudding is nicely puffed up and the top is golden.

Apulia   **TIELLA**   Serves 4 to 6
                          Tiella

Tiella is a distant relative of the Spanish rice dish *paella* and dates back to the days when southern Italy was under Spanish rule. One of the main differences is that tiella is based on potatoes, one of Apulia's favourite vegetables. Sometimes both potatoes and rice are used. The rest of the ingredients vary from town to town.

65 ml (2½ fl oz) olive oil
2 garlic cloves, crushed
a handful of parsley, finely chopped
2 teaspoons fresh basil, or ½ teaspoon dried
2 large onions, thinly sliced
225 g (8 oz) mushrooms, thinly sliced
salt
freshly ground black pepper
900 g (2 lb) waxy potatoes
175 g (6 oz) Mozzarella cheese, thinly sliced
50 g (2 oz) freshly grated Parmesan cheese
25 g (1 oz) wholemeal breadcrumbs

Heat half of the olive oil in a large frying pan and cook the garlic, parsley, basil and onions over a moderate heat for 3 minutes. Add the mushrooms and continue to cook for another 5 minutes or until the mushrooms are tender.

Season with salt and black pepper and set aside.

Peel the potatoes and cook in lightly salted, boiling water for 10 to 12 minutes or until they are just tender. Allow to cool slightly and slice thinly.

Grease a large, shallow baking dish and spread half the potato slices over the bottom. Cover with half of the onions and mushrooms and sprinkle with salt and black pepper. Top with half of the Mozzarella cheese and sprinkle with Parmesan cheese. Repeat the layers, ending with slices of Mozzarella and a sprinkling of Parmesan cheese. Sprinkle the breadcrumbs over the top and dribble over the remaining olive oil. Bake in a preheated oven at 190°C (375°F/Gas Mark 5) for 30 to 40 minutes or until the top is golden.

| Lombardy | **CAULIFLOWER AND RICE CASSEROLE** | Serves 4 to 6 |

Crostata di riso e cavolfiore

1 medium cauliflower
1 tablespoon olive oil
1 small onion, finely chopped
1 teaspoon parsley, finely chopped
175g (6oz) long grain rice
450ml (¾ pint) boiling stock or water
½ teaspoon salt
25g (1oz) butter
40g (1½oz) freshly grated Parmesan cheese
350ml (12fl oz) béchamel sauce (see page 57)
40g (1½oz) grated Gruyère cheese

Cut away the stem of the cauliflower and break the curd into florets. Steam for 10 minutes or until tender.

Heat the olive oil in a small saucepan and cook the onion and parsley over a moderate heat for 3 minutes. Stir in the rice and cook for 1 minute, so each grain is coated with oil. Add the boiling stock or water and salt, cover and simmer for 8 to 10 minutes until the rice is tender but still firm. Remove from the heat and stir in the butter and

25g (1oz) of the grated Parmesan cheese. Prepare the béchamel sauce, remove from the heat and stir in the Gruyère cheese.

Spread a layer of rice in the bottom of a well-buttered, shallow baking dish. Spoon a little of the cheese sauce over the rice. Cover with a layer of cauliflower. Repeat the layers, ending with the cheese sauce. Sprinkle the top with the remaining grated Parmesan and bake in a preheated oven at 190°C (375°F/Gas Mark 5) for 20 to 25 minutes or until the top is golden.

Emilia-Romagna and the North	**BROCCOLI GRATIN** *Broccoli gratinati*	Serves 4

1 head broccoli (about 450g (1lb))
450ml (¾ pint) béchamel sauce (see page 57)
40g (1½oz) freshly grated Parmesan cheese
2 tablespoons wholemeal breadcrumbs or wheatgerm
25g (1oz) butter

Trim the stalk of the broccoli. Break the head into florets and cut the stalks into bite-size pieces. Steam for 8 minutes or until just tender.

Prepare the béchamel sauce, remove from the heat and stir in 25g (1oz) grated Parmesan cheese. Pour some of the sauce into the bottom of a shallow baking dish. Cover with broccoli and pour over the remaining sauce. Mix the breadcrumbs with the remaining grated cheese and sprinkle over the top of the sauce. Dot with butter and bake in a preheated oven at 190°C (375°F/Gas Mark 5) for 25 to 30 minutes or until the top is golden.

Valle d'Aosta	**POTATO PIE** *Tortino di patate*	Serves 6

40g (1½oz) butter
1.5kg (3lb) potatoes, peeled and thinly sliced

1 large onion, thinly sliced
75g (3oz) grated Gruyère cheese;
50g (2oz) freshly grated Parmesan cheese
450ml (¾ pint) milk (or half milk and half stock)
¼ teaspoon freshly grated nutmeg
salt
freshly ground black pepper

Use 15g (½oz) butter to grease a large baking dish and arrange half of the potatoes on the bottom. Cover with half of the onions, then half of the Gruyère cheese and sprinkle with half of the Parmesan cheese. Repeat with the remaining potatoes, onions and Gruyère cheese. Bring the milk to just below simmering point. Add the nutmeg with salt and black pepper to taste and pour into the baking dish. Sprinkle the top with the remaining Parmesan cheese and dot with the remaining butter.

Cover loosely with foil and bake in a preheated oven at 180°C (350°F/Gas Mark 4) for 15 minutes. Remove the foil and bake for a further 50 to 60 minutes or until the potatoes are tender and the top is golden.

FRITTERS AND CROQUETTES
Bigne e crocchette

Italians love fritters and croquettes. Most regions of Italy make a *fritto misto* or 'mixed fry'. A wide variety of ingredients are used, such as aubergine, courgettes, potato or rice, Ricotta cheese and fried artichokes. They make a delicious light supper served with a green salad on the side.

A light vegetable oil such as peanut or corn oil is best for deep-frying. Safflower or sunflower oils are unsuitable for deep-frying. The oil should be heated to about 360°F before the fritters are added. To test for the correct heat, drop a morsel of bread into the hot oil. When it turns golden the oil is ready to be used.

Do not overcrowd the fritters when cooking. Leave

plenty of room for them to puff out. The first batch of fritters may be kept warm in a preheated 180°C (350°F/ Gas Mark 4) oven while the next batch is cooking.

FRITTER BATTER
Pastella per bigne
Makes about 450ml (¾ pint)

200g (7oz) wholemeal or plain white flour
½ teaspoon salt
1 egg
2 tablespoons olive oil
about 225ml (8fl oz) water

Mix the flour, salt, egg and olive oil in a bowl. Gradually stir in the water to form a smooth batter the consistency of heavy cream. Let rest 1 hour before using.

Umbria ## CARDOON FRITTERS PERUGIA STYLE Serves 4
Cardi alla perugina

Cardoons are members of the thistle family. The long fleshy stalks and ribs, that are similar to celery, are the parts used. Like artichokes they should be dropped in acidulated water or rubbed with lemon juice when cut to prevent them discolouring.

900g (2lb) cardoons, trimmed of their leaves
juice of 1 lemon above
450ml (¾ pint) fritter batter (see above)
oil for deep frying
450ml (¾ pint) mushroom and tomato sauce (see page 56)
225g (8oz) Mozzarella cheese, thinly sliced
50g (2oz) freshly grated Parmesan cheese

Trim the outer stalks of the cardoons and remove any stringy parts as you would for celery. Cut the remaining stalks into 5cm (2 inch) lengths and drop into acidulated water (add the juice of 1 lemon to 900ml (1½ pints) water). Steam for about 1½ hours or until they are tender. Dip the cardoons in the batter and fry in hot oil until golden on both sides. Drain on a paper towel.

Prepare the mushroom and tomato sauce and spoon a layer of the sauce into the bottom of a well-greased baking dish. Cover with a layer of cardoon fritters, top with slices of Mozzarella cheese and sprinkle with grated Parmesan. Bake in a preheated oven at 200°C (400°F/Gas Mark 6) for 20 minutes or until the top is golden.

Apulia   **AUBERGINE AND**   Serves 6
MOZZARELLA FRITTERS
Fritto di melanzane filanti

2 medium aubergines (about 675g (1½lb))
salt
225g (8oz) Ricotta cheese
100g (4oz) Mozzarella cheese, cut into small dice
50g (2oz) freshly grated Parmesan cheese
1 tablespoon fresh parsley, finely chopped
1 egg yolk
freshly ground black pepper
450ml (¾ pint) fritter batter (see page 158)
oil for deep frying

Peel the aubergines and cut them crosswise into slices 5mm (¼ inch) thick. Sprinkle with salt, set in a colander and leave for 1 hour to release the bitter juices. Wash off the salt and pat the slices dry with a paper towel.

In a bowl combine the Ricotta, Mozzarella and Parmesan cheeses with the parsley and egg yolk. Season with salt and black pepper to taste and mix well. Sandwich a little of this filling between 2 slices of aubergine. Repeat until you have used up all the aubergine and filling. Press the edges firmly together with a fork and dip into the fritter batter. Fry in hot oil until golden on both sides. Drain on a paper towel and serve at once.

Lazio   **RICOTTA CHEESE**   Serves 4
FRITTERS
Doratini di ricotta

These crisp, light fritters could not be simpler to prepare. This is a very versatile dish that is perfect as an antipasto with cocktails, or as a light luncheon or supper dish.

450g (1lb) Ricotta cheese
4 egg yolks
50g (2oz) freshly grated Parmesan cheese
40g (1½oz) flour
⅛ teaspoon freshly grated nutmeg
salt
freshly ground black pepper
flour for dusting
oil for deep frying

Combine the Ricotta cheese, egg yolks, grated Parmesan cheese and flour in a bowl. Add the nutmeg with salt and black pepper to taste. Blend well together. Form into small balls the size of a walnut. Roll in flour and fry in hot oil until golden. Drain on a paper towel and serve at once.

All Italy   **MIXED FRY**   Serves 6
Fritto misto

Each region of Italy makes its own combination of mixed fry. I have selected a typical vegetable combination but you may include any of the following: artichoke hearts, asparagus tips, beetroot, broccoli, cardoons, celery, aubergine, scorzonera (oyster plant), and green tomatoes.

225g (8oz) wholemeal or plain white flour
½ teaspoon salt
2 eggs, separated
2 tablespoons olive oil
2 tablespoons brandy
about 250ml (8floz) water
225g (8oz) broccoli

1 fennel bulb, trimmed and cut into strips
2 small courgettes, sliced
225g (8oz) button mushrooms
oil for deep frying
1 lemon, cut into wedges

Combine the flour and salt in a bowl and make a well in the centre. Add the egg yolks, olive oil and brandy. Stir in the water to form a smooth batter. Allow to stand for 1 hour.

Trim the stalks of the broccoli and cut it into sections. Steam with the fennel strips for 8 to 10 minutes until both vegetables are just tender. Meanwhile, trim the courgettes and cut into quarters lengthwise. Wash the mushrooms and pat dry.

Beat the egg whites until stiff and fold into the batter. Dip all the vegetables into the batter and fry in hot oil until golden on both sides. Do not overcrowd while frying or the fritters will not be crisp. Drain in a paper towel. When all the fritters are cooked, serve at once, garnished with the lemon wedges.

Campania   **AUBERGINE FRITTERS**   Serves 4 to 6
Bigne di melanzane

Aubergine fritters are so delicious that I have included another simpler version.

2 medium aubergines (about 675g (1½lb))
salt
450ml (¾ pint) fritter batter (see page 158)
oil for deep frying

Peel the aubergines and cut them into slices about 1 cm (½ inch) thick. Sprinkle with salt and set in a colander for 1 hour to release the bitter juices. Wash off the salt and pat the slices dry.

Dip the slices into the fritter batter and fry in hot oil until golden on both sides. Drain on a paper towel and serve at once.

161

Friuli and **FENNEL FRITTERS** Serves 4
Venezia Giulia *Fritole di fenoci*

4 fennel bulbs
120 ml (4 fl oz) vinaigrette sauce (see page 60)
450 ml (¾ pint) fritter batter (see page 158)
oil for deep frying

Remove the outer leaves and stalks from the fennel bulbs. Trim the bases and cut into wedges. Steam the pieces for 20 to 30 minutes or until they are just tender. Transfer to a bowl and pour over the vinaigrette sauce. Leave to marinate for 1 hour.

Dip the fennel wedges into the batter and fry in hot oil until golden. Drain on a paper towel and serve at once.

Trentino **BEAN PATTIES** Serves 4
Polpettine di fagioli

350 g (12 oz) cooked dried white beans
2 tablespoons minced onion
1 egg
2 tablespoons freshly grated Parmesan cheese
a pinch of ground cloves
salt
freshly ground black pepper
approximately 40 g (1½ oz) wheatgerm
oil for deep frying

Force the beans through a sieve into a mixing bowl, or purée in a food processor. Add the onion, egg, Parmesan cheese, cloves and salt and black pepper to taste. Stir in the wheatgerm and blend well. The mixture should be firm enough to hold its shape. If the mixture is too soft, add a little more wheatgerm. Form into patties about 5 cm (2 in) in diameter and 1 cm (½ in) thick. Coat with wheatgerm and fry in hot oil (360°F) until golden on both sides.

Valle d'Aosta   **POTATO PANCAKE**   Serves 2 to 3
Fritelle di patate

A children's favourite.

450g (1 lb) potatoes
2 tablespoons wholemeal or plain white flour
25g (1 oz) freshly grated Parmesan cheese
1 egg
a handful of parsley, finely chopped
2 tablespoons fresh basil, finely chopped
salt
freshly ground black pepper
3 tablespoons olive oil

Peel the potatoes and grate them on a coarse grater into a mixing bowl. Add the flour, Parmesan, egg, parsley, basil, salt and black pepper to taste and mix well.

Heat the olive oil in a large frying pan with a flameproof handle. Put in the potato mixture and spread out evenly in one layer. Cook gently for 15 minutes until the bottom is nicely browned. Turn the grill to high and set the frying pan so it is about 30 cm (12 inches) away from the grill. Grill for 8 to 10 minutes until the top of the pancake is golden. Serve at once.

Lazio   **STUFFED POTATO CROQUETTES**   Serves 4
Crocchette di patate con mozzarella

900g (1½lb) potatoes, peeled
3 eggs
50g (2oz) wholemeal flour
25g (1oz) freshly grated Parmesan cheese
⅛ teaspoon freshly grated nutmeg
salt
freshly ground black pepper
100g (4oz) Mozzarella cheese, cut into small cubes
flour for dusting
dry breadcrumbs
oil for deep frying

Boil the potatoes in lightly salted water for 20 minutes or until they are tender. Drain and press through a sieve into a mixing bowl. Add 1 egg and blend well. Stir in the wholemeal flour, Parmesan cheese, nutmeg and salt and black pepper to taste.

Form into small balls the size of a lime. Punch a deep hole into each one with the forefinger and place a cube of Mozzarella into the centre. Cover with a little potato mixture so the filling is completely encased. Roll in flour, dip in the remaining eggs, beaten, then roll in breadcrumbs. Fry in hot oil until crisp and golden.

Lazio   **RICE CROQUETTES**   Serves 4 to 6
WITH CHEESE AND
MUSHROOMS
Supplì al telefono con funghi

In Rome *supplì* are made with Provatura cheese which is made from buffalo's milk. Mozzarella makes a perfect substitute. They are called 'telephone' croquettes because the hot melted cheese hangs like a telephone wire around your face when you bite into them.

2 tablespoons olive oil
1 garlic clove, crushed
a handful of parsley, finely chopped
a few leaves of fresh mint, or ⅛ teaspoon dried
225g (8oz) mushrooms, chopped
350g (12oz) cooked rice
2 eggs
salt
freshly ground black pepper
40g (1½oz) Mozzarella cheese, cut into small cubes
wholemeal flour
dry breadcrumbs
oil for deep frying

Heat the olive oil in a frying pan and cook the garlic, parsley and mint for 1 minute. Add the mushrooms and cook over a moderate heat for 5 minutes. Set aside to cool slightly.

Place the cooked rice in a mixing bowl and add 1 egg and salt and black pepper to taste. Mix well. Moisten your hands with cold water and shape the rice into balls the size of a lemon. With your forefinger punch a hole into the centre. Place a teaspoon of the mushroom mixture and a cube of Mozzarella into each hole. Cover the cheese with rice so it is completely enclosed.

Roll in wholemeal flour, dip in the remaining egg, beaten, then roll in breadcrumbs. Fry in hot oil until crisp and golden.

Apulia   **COURGETTE**   Serves 4
                CROQUETTES
Polpettone di zucchini

3 medium potatoes
1 egg, beaten
2 courgettes, grated
1 large onion, grated
750g (3oz) freshly grated Parmesan cheese
1 slice of wholemeal bread, about 2.5cm (1 inch) thick
120ml (4floz) milk
⅛ teaspoon freshly grated nutmeg
salt
freshly ground black pepper
oil for deep frying

Boil the potatoes in lightly salted water for 20 minutes or until they are tender. Drain and press through a sieve into a mixing bowl. Add the beaten egg, grated courgette, onion and grated Parmesan and blend well.

Remove the crusts from the slice of bread and soak it in the milk. Squeeze dry and add to the potato mixture. Season with nutmeg and salt and black pepper to taste.

Form into small balls the size of a lime and fry in hot oil until golden.

STUFFED VEGETABLES
Legumi imbottite

Italians love stuffed vegetables. Aubergines, courgettes, peppers, onions, mushrooms and tomatoes are the most usual vegetables to be stuffed. There are probably as many different versions of each as there are cooks.

Stuffed vegetables make an excellent main course, but if you use smaller quantities, they may also be served as appetizers or side vegetables.

Liguria   **STUFFED COURGETTES**   Serves 3
WITH MUSHROOMS
Zucchini ripieni

The courgettes are filled with a delicate stuffing of onions, mushrooms, herbs and grated cheese. Sometimes dried mushrooms are used instead.

9 medium courgettes
2 tablespoons olive oil
1 garlic clove, crushed
a handful of parsley, finely chopped
1 tablespoon fresh marjoram or ½ teaspoon dried
1 small onion, finely chopped
100g (4oz) mushrooms, chopped
40g (1½oz) wholemeal breadcrumbs, soaked in 120ml
  (4floz) milk
75g (3oz) freshly grated Parmesan cheese
1 egg, beaten
salt
freshly ground black pepper
25g (1oz) butter

Steam the courgettes for 10 minutes or until they are just tender. Cool slightly. Cut in half lengthwise and scoop out the flesh with an apple corer, leaving the shells 5mm (¼ inch) thick. Chop the flesh of the courgettes.

Heat the olive oil in a frying pan and cook the garlic,

parsley and marjoram for 1 minute. Add the onion and cook over a moderate heat for 5 minutes. Add the chopped courgette and the mushrooms and continue to cook until the vegetables are tender and turning golden. Place the onion mixture, the breadcrumbs soaked in milk, half the Parmesan cheese, the egg, and salt and black pepper to taste in a bowl and mix together well.

Stuff the courgette shells with the mixture. Sprinkle with the remaining grated cheese and dot with butter. Arrange side by side on a well-greased baking sheet. Bake in a preheated oven at 180°C (350°F/Gas Mark 4) for 30 minutes or until the tops are golden.

| Tuscany | **STUFFED COURGETTES FLORENTINE** | Serves 4 |

Zucchini ripieni alla fiorentina

This is an elegant dish, which is perfect for a dinner party. The courgettes are stuffed with a mixture of spinach, herbs and cheese, topped with a béchamel sauce and grated cheese, and baked in the oven until the tops are golden. The dish may be prepared ahead of time and baked in the oven just before serving.

8 small courgettes
225g (8oz) spinach
2 tablespoons olive oil
1 garlic clove, crushed
2 tablespoons parsley, finely chopped
100g (4oz) freshly grated Parmesan cheese
⅛ teaspoon freshly grated nutmeg
salt
freshly ground black pepper
450ml (¾ pint) béchamel sauce (see page 57)

Steam the courgettes for 10 minutes or until they are just tender. Cool slightly. Cut in half lengthwise and scoop out the flesh with an apple corer, leaving the shells 5mm (¼ inch) thick. Chop the flesh of the courgettes.

Wash the spinach carefully and cook in a covered saucepan over a moderate heat for 5 minutes. The water clinging to the leaves is sufficient to prevent scorching. Drain and chop coarsely.

Heat the olive oil in a frying pan and cook the garlic and parsley for 1 minute. Add the chopped courgette and cook over a moderately high heat for 5 minutes or until tender and turning golden. Add the chopped spinach, 25 g (1 oz) Parmesan cheese, nutmeg and salt and black pepper to taste and mix well.

Spoon the mixture into the courgette halves and place side by side in a well-greased shallow baking dish. Prepare the béchamel sauce, remove from the heat and stir in 50 g (2 oz) of the grated Parmesan cheese. Pour the sauce over the stuffed courgettes and sprinkle with the remaining grated cheese. Bake in a preheated oven at 200°C (400°F/ Gas Mark 6) for 15 to 20 minutes or until the top is golden.

Campania   **STUFFED AUBERGINES**   Serves 4
WITH ALMONDS   to 6
Melanzane imbottite con mandorle

3 small aubergines (about 225 g (8 oz) each)
50 ml (2 fl oz) olive oil
1 garlic clove, crushed
1 onion, chopped
a handful of fresh parsley, finely chopped
2 teaspoons fresh oregano, or ½ teaspoon dried
3 or 4 plum tomatoes, peeled, seeded and chopped
40 g (1½ oz) shelled almonds, finely ground in a blender
15 g (½ oz) wholemeal breadcrumbs
salt
freshly ground black pepper
40 g (1½ oz) freshly grated Parmesan cheese

Place the aubergines in a saucepan of boiling water. Cover and simmer for 5 minutes. Remove and cut in half length-wise. Scoop out the pulp, taking care not to damage the skins, to leave a shell 3mm (⅛ inch) thick. Chop the pulp coarsely.

Heat the olive oil in a frying pan and cook the garlic, onion, parsley and oregano over a moderate heat for 3 minutes. Add the chopped aubergine and tomatoes. Cover and simmer for 10 to 15 minutes or until the aubergine is tender. Remove from the heat and stir in the ground almonds, breadcrumbs and salt and black pepper to taste. Fill the aubergine shells with the mixture and sprinkle the grated cheese on top.

Place side by side on a well-greased shallow baking dish and bake in a preheated oven at 180°C (350°F/Gas Mark 4) for 30 minutes or until the top is nicely browned.

| All Italy | **PEPPERS STUFFED WITH RICE AND PINE NUTS** *Peperoni imbottite* | Serves 3 to 4 |

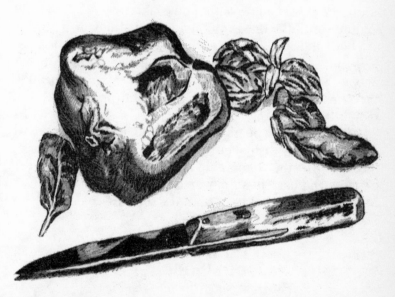

Stuffed peppers are made all over Italy. This recipe has a simple rice stuffing flavoured with tomato sauce, herbs and pine nuts, which give it a delicious nutty flavour.

6 to 8 red or green peppers
4 tablespoons olive oil
1 small onion, chopped
1 tablespoon fresh basil, or ¼ teaspoon dried
2 tablespoons fresh parsley, finely chopped
175 g (6 oz) long grain rice
600 ml (1 pint) boiling water
450 ml (¾ pint) tomato sauce (see page 54)
25 g (1 oz) pine nuts
50 g (2 oz) freshly grated Parmesan cheese
salt
freshly ground black pepper

Wash the peppers and place in a saucepan of boiling water. Cover, and simmer for 5 minutes. Cut in half lengthwise and remove the seeds and pith.

Heat 2 tablespoons of olive oil in a saucepan and cook the onion, basil and parsley for 3 minutes. Add the rice and cook for 1 minute, so the grains are well coated. Add 450 ml (¾ pint) boiling water and cook, covered for 15 to 20 minutes until the rice is just tender but still firm. Transfer to a bowl and combine with 120 ml (4 fl oz) tomato sauce, the pine nuts, 25 g (1 oz) Parmesan cheese, salt and black pepper. Stuff the pepper halves with the mixture. Sprinkle the remaining grated cheese on top and dribble over the remaining olive oil.

Arrange the peppers side by side in a well-greased shallow baking dish. Pour the rest of the tomato sauce, mixed with the remaining boiling water, around the peppers and bake in a preheated oven at 180°C (350°F/Gas Mark 4) for 30 minutes or until the tops are golden.

Sicily   **SICILIAN STUFFED**   Serves 6
PEPPERS
Peperoni imbottite alla siciliana

Stuffed peppers are a very versatile dish. They may be served as an antipasto or light main course, and are especially good for a buffet, as they can be served hot or at room temperature. The sweet and sharp combination of sultanas, pine nuts, olives and capers is typical of Sicilian cooking.

6 green or red peppers
75g (3oz) wholemeal breadcrumbs
3 tablespoons pine nuts
3 tablespoons sultanas
2 tablespoons capers
50g (2oz) Italian or Greek black olives, stoned and chopped
50ml (2fl oz) olive oil
15g (½oz) fresh parsley, finely chopped
2 teaspoons fresh basil, or ½ teaspoon dried
salt
freshly ground black pepper
450ml (¾ pint) tomato sauce (see page 54)
120ml (4fl oz) boiling water

Wash the peppers, cut them in half and remove the seeds and pith. In a bowl combine the breadcrumbs, pine nuts, sultanas, capers, olives, olive oil, parsley, basil and salt and black pepper to taste and blend well together. Stuff the peppers with the mixture and arrange side by side in a well-greased, shallow baking dish. Pour the tomato sauce, mixed with the boiling water, around the peppers and bake in a preheated oven at 180°C (350°F/Gas Mark 4) for 1 hour or until the tops are golden. If the liquid dries out during cooking, add a little more water.

Emilia-Romagna **STUFFED** Serves 4 to 6
and the North **MUSHROOM CAPS**
Funghi imbottite

24 large mushrooms
about 120ml (4fl oz) olive oil
2 garlic cloves, crushed
1 small onion, finely chopped
a handful of parsley, finely chopped
1 teaspoon fresh oregano, or ¼ teaspoon dried
a pinch of thyme

50g (2oz) wholemeal breadcrumbs
40g (1¼oz) freshly grated Parmesan cheese
⅛ teaspoon freshly grated nutmeg
salt
freshly ground black pepper

Wash the mushrooms, remove the stems and arrange the caps side by side in a well-greased, shallow baking dish. Chop the stems finely and set aside.

Heat 50 ml (2 fl oz) olive oil in a frying pan and cook the garlic, onion, mushroom stems, parsley, oregano and thyme over a moderate heat for 5 minutes. Remove from the heat and stir in the breadcrumbs, grated Parmesan, nutmeg, salt and black pepper.

Stuff the mushroom caps with the mixture and sprinkle with the remaining olive oil. Bake in a preheated oven at 180°C (350°F/Gas Mark 4) for 20 minutes or until the tops are golden.

Liguria   **STUFFED TOMATOES**   Serves 2 to 4
Pomodori al forno

This unusual recipe for stuffed tomatoes makes a delicious light lunch or supper dish.

4 large firm tomatoes
225g (8oz) Swiss chard or spinach
175g (6oz) Ricotta cheese
1 egg
25g (1oz) freshly grated Parmesan cheese
a handful of parsley, finely chopped
1 teaspoon fresh marjoram, or ¼ teaspoon dried
3 tablespoons olive oil
salt
freshly ground black pepper
15g (½oz) wholemeal breadcrumbs

Cut the tomatoes in half crosswise and scoop out most of the pulp and seeds, leaving shells about 5mm (¼ inch) thick.

Wash the Swiss chard or spinach and cook in a covered saucepan over a moderate heat for 6 minutes. The water clinging to the leaves is sufficient to prevent scorching. Drain, squeeze dry and chop finely.

Combine the Ricotta cheese, egg, Parmesan cheese, Swiss chard or spinach, parsley, marjoram and 1 table-spoon of olive oil in a mixing bowl and blend well together. Season with salt and black pepper.

Stuff the tomato halves with the mixture. Sprinkle the tops with breadcrumbs and dribble the remaining olive oil over the top. Arrange in a well-greased baking dish and bake in a preheated oven at 180°C (350°F/Gas Mark 4) for 30 to 35 minutes or until the tops are golden and the tomatoes are tender but still retain their shape.

CRÊPES
Crespelle

Crêpes make delicious, versatile main courses. They may be filled with vegetables of all kinds or any of the fillings for stuffed pasta, topped with sauce, and browned under the grill or in a hot oven.

Crêpe batter should be made at least 2 hours before cooking. The batter will need to be mixed again before using. If it has thickened, a little more water should be added to make it the consistency of thin cream.

A heavy cast-iron pan with sloping sides is best for crêpes – about 12.5 or 15 cm (5 or 6 inches) in diameter. To keep crêpes warm place them between two soup plates and set on top of a saucepan of simmering water. Crêpes can be stored for up to 2 days in the refrigerator or frozen for up to 2 months if well wrapped.

All Italy **CRÊPE BATTER** Makes 15 crêpes
Pasta per crespelle

200g (7oz) wholemeal or plain white flour
3 eggs
a pinch of salt
about 400ml (14 floz) water (or half milk and half water)
2 tablespoons olive oil

Place the flour in a bowl. Make a well in the centre and drop in the eggs and salt. Mix well with a wooden spoon. Gradually add the water, beating constantly to form a smooth batter the consistency of thin cream. Allow to stand at least 2 hours before using.

Heat a little olive oil in a 15cm (6 inch) heavy frying pan. When it is hot, pour in 2½ to 3 tablespoons batter. Quickly tilt the pan in all directions so the batter evenly covers the pan. Cook for about 1 minute on each side. Slide on to a soup plate and keep them warm as described above. Lightly oil the pan again and repeat until the batter is used up.

Abruzzi   **STUFFED PANCAKES**   Serves 4 to 5
                 WITH PEAS
               Scripelle 'mbusse

There are many versions of *scripelle 'mbusse* in the
Abruzzi. The stuffing and sauce may vary but peas are
always included.

350g (12oz) young, tender shelled peas
250ml (8fl oz) béchamel sauce (see page 57)
100g (4oz) freshly grated Parmesan cheese
15 crêpes (see page 174)
450ml (³⁄₄ pint) mushroom and tomato sauce (see page 56)

Cook the peas in a little water for 10 to 12 minutes or until
they are tender. The exact time will depend on the size and
age of the peas.
    Prepare the béchamel sauce. Stir in 40g (1¹⁄₂oz) grated
Parmesan cheese and the peas. Spoon a little filling into
each crêpe and roll them up. Arrange the crêpes in a single
layer in a well-greased, shallow baking dish. Cover with the
mushroom and tomato sauce and bake in a preheated oven
at 190°C (375°F/Gas Mark 5) until the crêpes are heated
through. Just before serving, sprinkle with a little grated
Parmesan and serve with the remaining grated Parmesan
on the side.

Emilia-   **COURGETTE FILLED**   Serves 4 to 5
Romagna   **CRÊPES**
          Crespelle imbottite con zucchine

This is a simple but elegant main course. Mushrooms
make a very good variation.

3 small courgettes
3 tablespoons olive oil
350ml (12fl oz) béchamel sauce (see page 57)
75g (3oz) freshly grated Parmesan cheese
15 crêpes (see page 174)
250ml (8floz) hot vegetable stock.
40g (1¹⁄₂oz) butter, melted

Trim the courgettes and cut them into thin slices. Heat the olive oil in a large frying pan and quickly fry the courgettes until they are golden on both sides. Drain on a paper towel.

Prepare the béchamel sauce and stir in half the Parmesan cheese and the fried courgettes. Spoon a little filling into the centre of each crêpe and roll them up. Arrange the crêpes in a single layer in a well-greased, shallow baking dish. Pour in the hot stock, sprinkle with the remaining Parmesan cheese and dribble over the melted butter.

Bake in a preheated oven at 190°C (375°F/Gas Mark 5) for 15 minutes or until the crêpes are heated through and the stock, Parmesan cheese and butter have combined to make a light sauce.

Campania   **CRÊPES WITH CHEESE**   Serves 4
       AND PARSLEY FILLING   to 6
Crespelle imbottite con ricotta

225g (8oz) Ricotta cheese
2 eggs
225g (8oz) Mozzarella cheese, cut into small dice
100g (4oz) freshly grated Parmesan cheese
a handful of parsley, finely chopped
salt
freshly ground black pepper
15 crêpes (see page 174)
450ml (¾ pint) tomato sauce (see page 54)

In a mixing bowl combine the Ricotta cheese, eggs, Mozzarella, 50g (2oz) of the Parmesan cheese and parsley. Season to taste with salt and black pepper and blend well together. Spoon a little filling into the centre of each crêpe and roll them up.

Arrange the crêpes in a single layer in a well-greased, shallow baking dish. Pour over the tomato sauce and bake in a preheated oven at 190°C (375°F/Gas Mark 5) for 15 minutes or until the crêpes and sauce are heated through.

Just before serving, sprinkle with a little grated Parmesan
and serve with the remaining grated cheese on the side.

Emilia-   **SPINACH, CHEESE**   Serves 6
Romagna   **AND TOMATO CRÊPE**
                   CAKE
              Timballo di crespelle

675g (1½lb) spinach
50ml (2floz) double cream
⅛ teaspoon freshly grated nutmeg
salt
freshly ground black pepper
350ml (12floz) béchamel sauce (see page 57)
50g (2oz) grated Gruyère cheese
350g (12oz) Ricotta cheese
1 egg
2 tablespoons milk
350ml (12fl oz) tomato sauce (see page 54)
12 crêpes (see page 174)
50g (2oz) freshly grated Parmesan cheese

Wash the spinach and cook in a covered saucepan over a
moderate heat for 5 minutes. The water clinging to the
leaves is sufficient to prevent scorching. Drain and chop
coarsely. Combine the chopped spinach in a bowl with the
cream, nutmeg, salt and black pepper. Prepare the
béchamel sauce and remove from the heat. Stir in the
Gruyère cheese. Mix the Ricotta cheese with the egg and
milk and beat until smooth.

   Place a crêpe in the bottom of a well-buttered 1.7 litre (3
pint) soufflé dish. Spoon a third of the spinach mixture
over the crêpe and sprinkle with a little Parmesan cheese.
Cover with another crêpe and spoon over a third of the
cheese sauce. Cover with another crêpe and spoon over a
third of the Ricotta mixture. Top with another crêpe and
spoon over a third of the tomato sauce. Repeat the layers
until all the ingredients are used up. Finish with tomato
sauce and grated Parmesan cheese.

Bake in a preheated oven at 180°C (350°F/Gas Mark 4) for 30 to 40 minutes or until the top is golden and the sauce is bubbling. Serve cut into wedges like a cake.

EGGS
UOVA

FRITTATA
Frittata

The Italian *frittata* is similar to the Spanish omelette. It is flat and round and cooked on both sides like a pancake. It should not be creamy like a French omelette but firm and set.

Almost any cooked vegetable can be incorporated into a *frittata* together with grated cheese and herbs. Some *frittate* are thickened slightly with breadcrumbs or flour; some are baked in the oven like a pie.

To cook a *frittata*, heat a little olive oil in a heavy based frying pan with a flameproof handle. Add the egg mixture and cook until the bottom is nicely browned. Place the frying pan under a preheated grill for 20 seconds to set the top, then slide the *frittata* on to a saucepan lid or plate. Place the frying pan over the uncooked side of the *frittata* and hold it snugly against the saucepan lid. Quickly flip the saucepan lid over so the uncooked side of the *frittata* is on the bottom of the frying pan. Continue cooking the *frittata* on the hob until the bottom is golden. Slide it on to a serving platter and serve cut into wedges like a pie.

Friuli and Venezia Giulia	**LEEK, FENNEL AND PEA FRITTATA**	Serves 2 to 3

Fertae cui cesarons

This is a very tasty *frittata*.

2 tablespoons olive oil
1 onion, chopped
1 leek, cut into thin slices
1 fennel bulb, trimmed and cut into strips

1 teaspoon fresh mint, or ¼ teaspoon dried
175g (6oz) fresh shelled peas
4 eggs
¼ teaspoon salt
a grinding of fresh black pepper
25g (1oz) butter

Heat the olive oil in a heavy frying pan and cook the onion, leek, fennel and mint over a moderate heat for 5 minutes. Add the peas and 2 to 3 tablespoons water and simmer, covered, for 15 minutes or until the peas and fennel are just tender. Remove from the heat and allow to cool slightly.

Beat the eggs in a bowl with the salt and pepper and fold in the cooked vegetables. Heat the butter in a large, heavy frying pan and, when foaming, pour in the egg mixture. Cook over a moderate heat until the bottom is nicely browned. Place under a preheated grill for 20 seconds to set the top. Follow the directions for turning the *frittata* on page 179 and cook on the other side until the bottom is nicely browned.

Abruzzi   **POTATO AND ONION**   Serves 2 to 3
                      FRITTATA
                   Frittata di patate

450g (1 lb) potatoes, peeled
50 ml (2 fl oz) olive oil
1 large onion, thinly sliced
a pinch of hot red pepper flakes
4 eggs
¼ teaspoon salt

Bring the potatoes to the boil in lightly salted water and
cook for 15 minutes or until they are just tender. Drain,
cool slightly and cut into thin slices.

Heat half of the olive oil in a large frying pan and cook
the onion and hot pepper flakes over a moderate heat for 3
minutes. Add the potatoes and cook for 5 minutes or until
they start to turn golden. Remove from the heat.

Beat the eggs with the salt and fold in the onion and
potato mixture. Heat the remaining olive oil in a large,
heavy frying pan and pour in the egg mixture. Cook over a
moderate heat until the bottom is nicely browned. Place
under a preheated grill for 20 seconds to set the top. Follow
the directions for turning the *frittata* on page 179 and cook
on the other side until the bottom is nicely browned.

Veneto   **MUSHROOM FRITTATA**   Serves 2 to 3
                   Frittata con funghi

2 tablespoons olive oil
450g (1 lb) mushrooms, thinly sliced
2 tablespoons fresh parsley, finely chopped
1 teaspoon flour
2 tablespoons dry Marsala
4 eggs
salt
freshly ground black pepper
25g (1 oz) butter

Heat the olive oil in a frying pan and cook the mushrooms

and parsley over a moderate heat for 5 minutes. Add the flour and cook for 1 minute. Stir in the Marsala and cook for a further minute. Remove from the heat and allow to cool.

Beat the eggs in a mixing bowl with salt and black pepper to taste. Add the mushroom mixture and mix well. Heat the butter in a large, heavy frying pan and, when foaming, pour in the egg mixture. Cook over a moderate heat until the bottom is nicely browned. Place under a preheated grill for 20 seconds to set the top. Follow directions for turning the *frittata* on page 179 and cook on the other side until the bottom is nicely browned.

| Liguria | **SWISS CHARD FRITTATA** | Serves 3 |
| | *Frittata di bietole* | to 4 |

The Swiss chard can be varied with any of the following green leafy vegetables: spinach, kale, watercress, spring greens or beet leaves.

450g (1 lb) Swiss chard
25g (1 oz) butter
1 garlic clove, crushed
1 small onion, finely chopped
salt
freshly ground black pepper
⅛ teaspoon freshly grated nutmeg
50g (2 oz) freshly grated Parmesan cheese
4 eggs
*25g (1 oz) wholemeal breadcrumbs, soaked in 50 ml (2 fl oz)
   milk*
2 tablespoons olive oil

Wash the Swiss chard and remove the stalks. Cook in a covered saucepan over a moderate heat for 5 minutes. The water clinging to the leaves is sufficient to prevent scorching. Drain and chop coarsely.

Heat the butter in a small saucepan and cook the garlic and onion for 3 minutes. Add the Swiss chard and simmer for 5 minutes. Drain and chop coarsely. Season with salt, black pepper and nutmeg. Remove from the heat and stir in the Parmesan cheese. Beat the eggs well and fold in the Swiss chard mixture and breadcrumbs.

Heat the olive oil in a large frying pan and pour in the egg mixture. Cook over a moderate heat until the bottom is nicely browned. Place under a preheated grill for 20 seconds to set the top. Following the directions to turn the *frittata* on page 179 and cook on the other side until the bottom is nicely browned.

Sicily   **MILLASSATA**   Serves 2
                            Millassata

2 globe artichokes
½ lemon
100 g (4 oz) fresh asparagus
65 ml (2½ fl oz) olive oil
1 garlic clove, crushed
a handful of fresh parsley, finely chopped
65 ml (2½ fl oz) dry white wine
3 eggs
25 g (1 oz) freshly grated Parmesan cheese
salt
freshly ground black pepper

Trim the artichokes and remove the leaves and chokes as described on page 200. Cut bottoms of artichokes into slices 5 mm (¼ inch) thick and rub with lemon to prevent the artichokes from discolouring. Trim the ends of the asparagus and peel the stalks with a sharp knife or vegetable peeler up to 5 mm (2 inches) from the tips. Steam for 15 minutes or until they are tender.

Heat half the olive oil in a frying pan and cook the garlic and parsley for 1 minute. Add the artichokes and cook over a moderate heat for 5 minutes. Add the wine and cook until the wine has evaporated and the artichokes are lightly browned and tender.

Beat the eggs with the grated cheese and fold in the

cooked artichokes and asparagus. Season with salt and black pepper to taste. Heat the remaining oil in a large frying pan and pour in the egg mixture. Cook over a moderate heat until the bottom is nicely browned. Place under a preheated grill for 20 seconds until the top is set. Follow directions for turning the *frittata* on page 179. Cook on the other side until the bottom is nicely browned.

Campania	**ONION AND CHEESE**	Serves 2 to 3
	FRITTATA	

Frittata di cipolle e mozzarella

This may be served hot or cold and is perfect for a picnic.

50 ml (2 fl oz) olive oil
2 large onions, thinly sliced
2 teaspoons fresh basil, chopped, or ½ teaspoon dried
4 eggs
25 g (1 oz) Mozzarella cheese, cut into small dice
salt
freshly ground black pepper

Heat half the olive oil in a frying pan and cook the onions and basil over a moderate heat for 8 to 10 minutes or until they are turning golden. Remove from the heat and allow to cool slightly.

Beat the eggs with the Mozzarella cheese and season to taste with salt and black pepper. Stir in the onions. Heat the remaining olive oil in a large, heavy frying pan and pour in the egg mixture. Cook over a moderate heat until the bottom is nicely browned. Place under a preheated grill for 20 seconds until the top is set. Follow the directions for turning the *frittata* on page 179. Cook on the other side until the bottom is nicely browned.

Sardinia **BAKED COURGETTE** Serves 2
OMELETTE to 3
Frittata sardenaira

Baked omelettes are made all over Italy. They are easier to
prepare than soufflés or *sformati* and make a perfect dish
for an unexpected luncheon or supper.

3 medium courgettes (about 450g (1 lb))
50 ml (2 fl oz) olive oil
2 garlic cloves, crushed
2 teaspoons fresh basil, or ½ teaspoon dried
1 tablespoon fresh parsley, finely chopped
4 eggs
25g (1 oz) wholemeal breadcrumbs, soaked in 50 ml (2 fl oz)
milk
25g (1 oz) freshly grated Pecorino cheese
salt
freshly ground black pepper

Trim the courgettes and cut them into thin slices. Heat
the olive oil in a large frying pan and cook the garlic, basil
and parsley for 1 minute. Add the courgettes and cook
over a moderately high heat for 5 minutes until the courgettes are tender and starting to turn golden. Remove from
the heat and allow to cool slightly.

Beat the eggs well and stir in the breadcrumbs and
Pecorino cheese. Season to taste with salt and black
pepper. Fold in the cooked courgettes and pour into a well-
greased, shallow baking dish. Bake in a preheated 190°C
(375°F/Gas Mark 5) oven for 25 to 30 minutes or until the
top is golden and the centre is set. Serve at once.

Sardinia **BAKED PEA OMELETTE** Serves 2
Torta di piselli to 3

3 tablespoons olive oil
1 small onion, chopped
a handful of parsley, finely chopped
350g (12 oz) fresh shelled peas

4 eggs
25g (1oz) freshly grated Pecorino cheese
salt
freshly ground black pepper
25g (1oz) wholemeal breadcrumbs, soaked in 4 tablespoons
  milk

Heat the olive oil in a frying pan and cook the onion and parsley over a moderate heat for 3 minutes. Add the peas and 2 to 3 tablespoons water and simmer, covered, for 15 minutes or until the peas are tender.

Beat the eggs in a mixing bowl with the grated cheese. Season to taste with salt and black pepper. Stir in the breadcrumbs and the onion and pea mixture. Pour into a well-greased, shallow baking dish and bake in a preheated oven at 190°C (375°F/Gas Mark 5) for 25 to 30 minutes or until the top is golden and the centre is set. Serve at once.

Tuscany   **BAKED AUBERGINE**   Serves 3 to 4
                      OMELETTE
                 Tortino di melanzane

This is a speciality of Florence. *Tortino* literally means 'pie' or 'tartlet'. This *tortino* is very light and easy to prepare. For a variation, try it with potatoes or courgettes.

1 large aubergine (450–550g (1–1¼lb))
salt
120ml (4floz) olive oil
5 eggs
65ml (2½fl oz) tomato sauce (see page 54)
50g (2oz) freshly grated Parmesan cheese
freshly ground black pepper

Peel the aubergine and cut it into slices 3mm (⅛ inch) thick. Sprinkle with salt and set in a colander for 1 hour to release the bitter juices. Wash off the salt and pat the slices dry. Fry in hot olive oil until they are golden on both sides. Drain on a paper towel.

Beat the eggs in a bowl and add the tomato sauce and

Parmesan cheese. Season to taste with salt and black pepper.

Arrange the aubergine slices in the bottom of a well-greased, shallow baking dish. Pour over the egg mixture and bake in a preheated oven at 190°C (375°F/Gas Mark 5) for 30 to 40 minutes or until the top is golden and the centre is set. Serve at once.

Tuscany   **BAKED ARTICHOKE**   Serves 3 to 4
OMELETTE
Tortino di carciofi

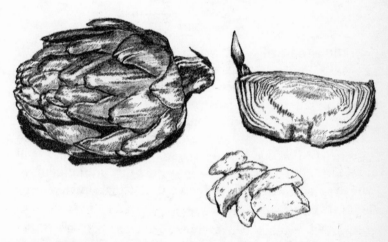

This delectable dish, like the *tortino di melanzane*, is a speciality of Florence. It is composed of deep-fried artichoke slices and beaten eggs baked in the oven like a pie, and it is well worth trying when artichokes are in season.

4 artichokes
1 lemon, cut in half
flour for dusting
oil for deep frying
4 eggs
2 tablespoons milk
salt
freshly ground black pepper

Trim the artichokes and remove the leaves and chokes as described on page 200. Cut bottoms of artichokes into slices 5mm (¼ inch) thick and rub with lemon to prevent discolouring. Dip in flour and fry in hot oil until golden on both sides. Drain on a paper towel.

Beat the eggs in a bowl with the milk, salt and black pepper. Arrange the fried artichokes in the bottom of a well-greased, shallow baking dish. Pour over the egg mixture and bake in a preheated oven at 190°C (375°F/Gas Mark 5) for 25 to 30 minutes or until the top is golden and the eggs are set.

SOUFFLÉS
Soffiati

A soufflé is basically a thick béchamel sauce mixed with egg yolks, a vegetable purée, grated cheese, or the flavouring of your choice. Stiffly beaten egg whites are folded in. The mixture is turned into a mould and baked in the oven until very puffed up and browned.

To make a light soufflé, the egg whites must be beaten into stiff peaks. Do not overbeat or the egg whites will become dry. Take care that the egg whites do not contain any particles of egg yolk or they will not rise satisfactorily. The best results are produced with a large wire whisk, but a hand beater or mixer is satisfactory. The bowl must be absolutely free of moisture or grease. Unlined copper produces the best results as the acid in the copper helps to stabilize the egg whites, but stainless steel or glass or porcelain make adequate substitutes.

Carefully fold a quarter of the egg whites into the warm sauce, then very lightly fold in the remaining egg whites. Turn into a well buttered soufflé dish and place in the centre of an oven preheated to 200°C (400°F/Gas Mark 6). Turn down the heat at once to 190°C 375°F/Gas Mark 5). Bake for 30 to 35 minutes until a knife comes out clean from the centre of the soufflé. Serve immediately as a cooked soufflé will start to sink rapidly after being removed from the oven.

Lombardy   **CHEESE SOUFFLÉ**   Serves 6
Soffiato di formaggii

50g (2oz) butter
50g (2oz) flour
350ml (12floz) hot milk
50g (2oz) grated Gruyère cheese
50g (2oz) freshly grated Parmesan cheese
¼ teaspoon freshly grated nutmeg
salt
freshly ground black pepper
6 egg yolks
7 egg whites

Follow the directions on page 57 and prepare a thick béchamel sauce using the butter, flour and hot milk. Remove from the heat and stir in the Gruyère and Parmesan cheeses, the nutmeg and salt and black pepper to taste. Add the egg yolks one at a time and mix well. Beat the egg whites until stiff and fold a quarter of the egg whites into the sauce. Blend well and lightly fold in the remaining egg whites.

Pour into a well-buttered 1.7 litre (3 pint) soufflé dish. Place in a preheated oven at 200°C (400°F/Gas Mark 6) and reduce the heat immediately to 190°C (375°F/Gas Mark 5). Bake for 30 to 35 minutes or until the soufflé is well risen and the centre is done. Serve at once.

Emilia-   **AUBERGINE SOUFFLÉ**   Serves 6
Romagna   *Soffiato di melanzane*

1 medium aubergine (about 350g (12oz))
salt
flour, for dusting
about 65ml (2½fl oz) olive oil
50g (2oz) butter
50g (2oz) flour
350ml (12floz) hot milk (or half milk and half stock)
75g (3oz) freshly grated Parmesan cheese
freshly ground black pepper

6 egg yolks
7 egg whites

Peel the aubergine and cut it into slices 5 mm (¼ inch) thick. Sprinkle with salt and leave for 1 hour to release the bitter juices. Wash off the salt and pat dry. Dip the aubergine slices in flour and fry in hot oil until golden on both sides. Force through a sieve or purée in a blender. There should be approximately 250–300 ml (8–10 fl oz) purée.

Follow the directions on page 57 and prepare a thick béchamel sauce using the butter, 5 tablespoons flour and hot milk. Remove from the heat and stir in the Parmesan cheese, aubergine purée and salt and black pepper to taste. Add the egg yolks, one at a time, and mix well. Beat the egg whites until stiff and fold a quarter of the egg whites into the sauce. Blend well and lightly fold in the remaining egg whites.

Pour into a well-buttered 1.7 litre (3 pint) soufflé dish. Place in the centre of a preheated oven at 200°C (400°F/Gas Mark 6) and immediately reduce the heat to 190°C (375°F/Gas Mark 5). Bake for 30 to 35 minutes or until the soufflé is well risen and the centre is done. Serve at once.

Emilia-Romagna   **SPINACH AND MUSHROOM SOUFFLÉ**   Serves 6
Soffiato di spinaci e funghi

Soufflés can be made equally well with a béchamel sauce made with stock instead of milk. The result is deliciously savoury and very light. Try it with this tasty combination of spinach and mushrooms.

450 g (1 lb) spinach
2 tablespoons olive oil
225 g (8 oz) mushrooms, thinly sliced
50 g (2 oz) butter
50 g (2 oz) flour
350 ml (12 fl oz) hot vegetable stock
50 g (2 oz) freshly grated Parmesan cheese

¼ teaspoon freshly grated nutmeg
salt
freshly ground black pepper
6 egg yolks
7 egg whites

Wash the spinach and cook in a covered saucepan over a moderate heat for 5 minutes. Drain, squeeze dry and chop finely. Heat the olive oil in a frying pan and cook the mushrooms over a moderate heat for 5 minutes or until they are tender and all the liquid has evaporated.

Follow the directions on page 57 and prepare a thick béchamel sauce using the butter, flour and hot stock. Remove from the heat and stir in the Parmesan cheese, chopped spinach, mushrooms and nutmeg, with salt and black pepper to taste. Add the egg yolks, one at a time, and mix well. Beat the egg whites until stiff and fold a quarter of the egg whites into the sauce. Blend well and lightly fold in the remaining egg whites.

Pour into a well-buttered 1.7 litre (3 pint) soufflé dish. Place in the centre of a preheated oven at 200°C (400°F/ Gas Mark 6) and immediately reduce the heat to 190°C (375°F/Gas Mark 5). Bake for 30 to 35 minutes or until the soufflé is well risen and the centre is done. Serve at once.

MOULDED SOUFFLÉS
Sformati

Sformati are similar to ordinary soufflés except they do not contain as many eggs. They are always cooked in a mould which is set in a pan of hot water. They do not rise as high as ordinary soufflés, nor do they sink as quickly. *Sformati* are usually served unmoulded on to a serving dish.

Tuscany   **BROCCOLI MOULDED**   Serves 4
SOUFFLÉ
Sformato di broccoli

This is very light and good.

350g (12oz) broccoli florets
2 tablespoons olive oil
40g (1½oz) butter
40g (1½oz) flour
250ml (8floz) hot milk (or half milk and half stock)
25g (1oz) freshly grated Parmesan cheese
⅛ teaspoon freshly grated nutmeg
salt
freshly ground black pepper
4 eggs, separated

Steam the broccoli florets for 10 minutes or until they are just tender. Heat the olive oil in a frying pan and cook the broccoli over a moderate heat for 3 minutes. Force through a sieve or purée in a blender.

Follow the directions on page 57 and prepare a thick béchamel sauce using the butter, flour and hot milk. Remove from the heat and stir in the Parmesan cheese, broccoli purée, nutmeg and salt and black pepper to taste. Add the egg yolks, one at a time, and mix well. Beat the egg whites until stiff and fold a quarter of the egg whites into the sauce. Blend well and lightly fold in the remaining egg whites.

Pour into a well-buttered 1.5 litre (2½ pint) soufflé dish and set in a pan of hot water. Cook in the centre of a preheated oven at 180°C (350°F/Gas Mark 4) for 30 minutes or until a knife comes out clean from the centre.

Lazio   **MOULDED PEA SOUFFLÉ**   Serves 4
Sformato di piselli

1 tablespoon olive oil
1 garlic clove, crushed
a few leaves of fresh mint, or a pinch of dried

350g (12oz) fresh shelled peas
50g (1oz) butter
40g (1½oz) flour
250ml (8floz) hot milk
25g (1oz) freshly grated Parmesan cheese
salt
freshly ground black pepper
4 eggs, separated

Heat the olive oil in a saucepan and cook the garlic, parsley and mint for 1 minute. Add the peas and a little water and simmer, covered, for 15 minutes or until the peas are tender and the liquid has evaporated. Force through a sieve or purée in a blender.

Follow the directions on page 57 and prepare a thick béchamel sauce using the butter, flour and hot milk. Remove from the heat and stir in the Parmesan cheese with salt and black pepper to taste. Add the eggs, one at a time, and mix well. Beat the egg whites until stiff and fold a quarter of the egg whites into the sauce. Blend well and lightly fold in the remaining egg whites.

Pour into a well-buttered 1.5 litre (2½ pint) soufflé dish and set in a pan of hot water. Cook in the centre of a preheated oven at 180°C (350°F/Gas Mark 4) for 30 minutes or until a knife comes out clean from the centre. Serve at once.

CHEESE

FORMAGGIO

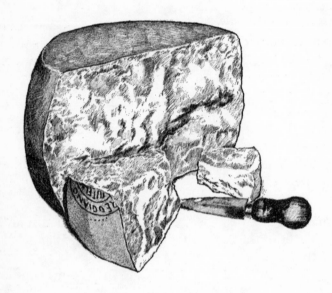

Cheese is frequently used in Italian cooking, in soups, pasta, rice, polenta and many vegetable dishes, but cheese cookery itself is limited. The cheeses most widely used for cooking are Parmesan, Pecorino, Mozzarella and Ricotta.

Parmesan cheese is probably the most famous of all Italian cheeses. Legally, cheese sold under this name is made in a carefully defined area around Parma and the neighbouring cities of Reggio and Piacenza. However, good Parmesan cheese is made in many regions of Italy and is sold under the name of Grana. Parmesan cheese is also excellent eaten as a sliced cheese. It comes in various qualities: Vecchio (old), which is two years old; Stravecchio (older), which is three years old; and the superior Stravecchione (extra old), which is at least four years old and can be aged for twenty years or even more. Parmesan cheese is extremely high in calcium – 100g (about 4oz) has as much calcium as 900 ml (1½ pints) milk. It is also very high in protein – weight for weight, sirloin steak has little more than two-thirds of the amount of protein found in Parmesan cheese. Good Parmesan should be light yellow in colour and sweat slightly. Always buy it whole and grate it just before using.

Pecorino or Pecorino Romano, as it is sometimes called, is another hard cheese which is similar to Parmesan and can be used for grating. It is made from ewes' milk and has a stronger flavour than Parmesan. Pecorino Sardo or Sardo is another type of Pecorino that is made in Sardinia. Asiago is a semi-fat hard cow's milk cheese that is also suitable for grating, when it is aged over 12 months. It is made in the province of Vincenza.

Mozzarella is a soft, white cheese used throughout Italy. It originated in Naples where it is made from buffalos' milk and eaten very fresh. Once it has dried out, it is only good for cooking. Elsewhere in Italy, Mozzarella is made from cows' milk. Fresh Mozzarella is generally lightly wrapped and stored in water. It is obtainable at most supermarkets and Italian grocers.

Another cheese frequently used in Italian cooking is Ricotta. It is a soft, fresh white cheese made from the whey of the milk. It is used in stuffings for various pasta dishes, and in cheesecakes and some desserts. Fresh Ricotta is easily obtainable at Italian grocers, delicatessens and many supermarkets. A commercial Ricotta made from cows' milk can be found in most supermarkets; it is a good substitute and keeps considerably longer.

Caciocavallo is another cheese that is used in cooking in the south and Sicily. It is made from buffalos' or cows' milk and has a strong spicy flavour, not unlike Provolone.

Fontina cheese is used extensively in cooking in Piedmont and the Valle d'Aosta where it is made. It is a soft, buttery cheese and is the basic ingredient of the famous Piedmontese dish *fonduta*.

Campania   **FRIED MOZZARELLA**   Serves 6
                             SANDWICHES
Mozzarella in carrozza

175g (6oz) Mozzarella cheese
6 slices wholemeal bread, cut in half
2 tablespoons milk
flour for dusting
2 eggs, beaten
120ml (4floz) olive oil

Cut the Mozzarella into thin slices and sandwich between the slices of bread. Sprinkle the sandwiches with milk and dip them in flour. Allow the sandwiches to soak in the beaten eggs, then press the edges together well to enclose the cheese securely.

Heat the olive oil in a frying pan and fry the sandwiches until golden on both sides. Serve at once.

Campania   **AUBERGINE AND**   Serves 4
               MOZZARELLA TOASTS
Crostini di melanzane e mozzarella

1 small aubergine (about 225g (8oz))
salt
65ml (2½floz) olive oil
120ml (4fl oz) tomato sauce (see page 54)
4 slices wholemeal bread, toasted
4 slices of Mozzarella cheese 3mm (⅛ inch) thick, cut the
     same size as the bread slices

Peel the aubergine and cut into slices 3mm (⅛ inch) thick. Sprinkle with salt and set in a colander for 1 hour to release the bitter juices. Wash off the salt and pat the slices dry with a paper towel. Fry in hot oil until golden on both sides. Drain on a paper towel.

Arrange the fried aubergine over the slices of toast. Spread a little tomato sauce over the aubergine and top with slices of Mozzarella cheese. Cook under a preheated hot grill until the cheese melts. Serve at once.

Lazio **CHEESE SKEWERS** Serves 6
Spiedini di provatura

Spiedini are the Italian equivalent of the French *brochettes* or skewers. They are morsels of food threaded on a skewer and grilled or deep fried. The skewers are usually 15 cm (6 inches) long and made of wood, stainless steel (or aluminium) or silver. Provatura cheese is a fresh buffalos' milk cheese made in the region around Rome. Mozzarella or Fontina cheese make good substitutes.

6 slices of wholemeal bread, cut into quarters
18 slices Provatura cheese, cut the same size as the bread
  quarters
3 or 4 plum tomatoes, cut into 18 slices 5 mm (¼ inch)
  thick
65 g (2½ oz) butter, melted
18 Italian or Greek black olives, to garnish

Thread the bread, cheese and tomato slices on to six skewers, beginning and ending with slices of bread. Cover the bottom of a baking dish with 3 tablespoons melted butter. Arrange the skewers on top. Sprinkle with the remaining melted butter.

Place under a preheated grill and cook them until they are golden, turning them so they cook evenly. Serve at once, garnished with black olives.

The North **CHEESE PUFFS** Serves 3
Bombole al formaggio

These very light fritters are equally good with cocktails, or as a light lunch dish with a green salad on the side. They may be served with tomato sauce.

3 egg whites
salt
100 g (4 oz) freshly grated Parmesan cheese
pinch of cayenne pepper
oil for deep frying

Beat the egg whites with a little salt until stiff. Gradually fold in the grated cheese and the cayenne pepper. Drop the mixture into hot oil a teaspoon at a time and fry until golden all over. Do not overcrowd. Drain on a paper towel and serve at once.

VEGETABLES
LEGUMI

The Italians have been master market gardeners since Roman times. Many vegetables that are grown throughout the western world were first cultivated in Italy, which is why many of them are still sometimes called by Italian names – broccoli, zucchini (courgettes), fava (broad) beans. Not only is the quality of vegetables in Italy unequalled in Europe, but because of the long growing season, vegetables are cheap and plentiful throughout the year.

Vegetables are always eaten fresh and when in season. They are stuffed, sautéed, baked, grilled, stewed, gratinéed or simply steamed and dressed with garlic, olive oil and lemon juice. They appear in soufflés, *frittate* (omelettes), puddings, tarts, with pasta or rice, and are, of course, the foundation of most Italian soups.

Herbs and spices of all kinds are used to enhance the natural flavour of the vegetables. Each region of Italy has its own special preferences: marjoram is the favourite herb of Piedmont; mint is typical of Roman cooking; Calabria uses large amounts of ginger; hot chilli peppers (*peperoncini*) flavour many of the vegetable dishes of the south and Sicily.

ARTICHOKES
Carciofi

Several varieties of artichokes are grown in Italy. One is long, narrow and purple, and is so tender that it can be eaten raw. Another is small and egg-shaped and is used for marinated artichokes. Also there is a large, round variety called *mamme* or *mammola*, that is similar to the globe artichoke found in many supermarkets.

Italians love artichokes and cook them in many different

ways. They may be boiled or steamed and served with a sauce on the side, stuffed, deep fried, stewed in wine and herbs, baked in a sauce, or served over pasta or risotto.

To steam or boil globe artichokes, cut off the top third of the leaves with a sharp knife or scissors and remove the stem. The heart or bottom will discolour quickly when cut, so rub at once with lemon juice. Never cook artichokes in an aluminium pan as it discolours them.

Veneto   **ARTICHOKES SIMMERED**   Serves 4
IN WINE
Carciofi alla veneziana

4 globe artichokes
1 lemon, cut in half
3 tablespoons olive oil
1 garlic clove, crushed
250 ml (8 fl oz) dry white wine

Cut off the top 5 cm (2 inches) of the artichokes, removing all the tough, inedible, dark green leaves. Trim the stems. Slice the artichokes in half lengthwise and remove the fuzzy choke. Slice the remaining hearts into slices 5 mm (¼ inch) thick. Rub all over with lemon to prevent the artichokes from turning black.

Heat the olive oil in a large frying pan and cook the garlic for 1 minute. Add the artichokes and cook over a moderate heat for 3 minutes. Add the wine, bring to the boil, cover and simmer for 15 minutes or until the artichokes are tender and the wine is reduced.

Sicily   **ARTICHOKES BRAISED**   Serves 6
WITH PEAS
AND POTATOES
Carciofi con piselli e patate

This is a rich and flavourful combination. Do not overcook, so the vegetables retain their distinctive flavours.

3 globe artichokes
½ lemon
3 tablespoons olive oil
2 garlic cloves, crushed
1 small onion, chopped
175g (6oz) fresh shelled peas
50ml (2fl oz) dry white wine (or water)
450g (1lb) small new potatoes, peeled
about 175ml (6fl oz) boiling water
salt
freshly ground black pepper

Trim the artichokes and remove the leaves and chokes as described opposite. Cut into very thin slices and rub all over with lemon to prevent the artichokes from discolouring

Heat the olive oil in a large frying pan and cook the garlic and onion over a moderate heat for 3 minutes. Add the artichoke slices and cook for a further 3 minutes. Add the peas and wine, bring to the boil, cover and simmer for 10 minutes.

If the potatoes are tiny, leave them whole, otherwise cut them into halves or quarters. Add to the artichokes and peas with the boiling water and season with salt and black pepper to taste. Cover and simmer for a further 15 to 20 minutes or until the potatoes are tender and the sauce is thickened.

Tuscany   **ARTICHOKES**   Serves 6
                 FLORENTINE
           Fondi di carciofi alla fiorentina

This dish may be served equally well as a side vegetable, main course or for a buffet. It can be prepared in advance and baked in the oven just before serving.

6 globe artichokes
900g (2lb) spinach
50g (2oz) butter
⅛ teaspoon freshly grated nutmeg

salt
freshly ground black pepper
450 ml (³⁄₄ pint) béchamel sauce (see page 57)
50 g (2 oz) freshly grated Parmesan cheese
3 tablespoons wholemeal breadcrumbs

Trim the stems of the artichokes and steam for 45 minutes to 1 hour or until the bottoms are tender and the outer leaves pull away easily. Set aside to cool.

Wash the spinach carefully and cook in a covered saucepan with 15 g (½ oz) butter. The water clinging to the leaves will be sufficient to prevent scorching. Drain and chop coarsely. Season with the nutmeg and salt and black pepper to taste.

Remove all the outer leaves and the fuzzy chokes from the artichokes. Slice the hearts 5 mm (¼ inch) thick and arrange in one layer in the bottom of a well-greased, shallow baking dish. Spread the cooked spinach over the top and cover with a layer of hot béchamel sauce mixed with 25 g (1 oz) Parmesan cheese. Combine the remaining Parmesan cheese with the breadcrumbs and sprinkle over the top. Dot with the remaining butter and bake in a preheated oven at 200°C (400°F/Gas Mark 6) for 20 minutes or until the top is golden.

Lombardy   **ASPARAGUS, LOMBARD STYLE**   Serves 4
Asparagii alla lombarda

Asparagus is usually eaten as an antipasto in Italy with a simple dressing of olive oil and lemon juice, or hot garlic-flavoured oil and grated cheese. *Asparagii alla lombarda* is usually listed on Italian menus under the *Piatti del Giorno* or 'Today's Specials' and served as a separate course. It may be served with fried or poached eggs.

675 g (1 ½ lb) asparagus
50 g (2 oz) freshly grated Parmesan cheese
50 g (2 oz) butter, melted
4 poached eggs

Trim the ends of the asparagus and peel the stalks with a
sharp knife or vegetable peeler up to about 5 cm (2 inches)
from the tips. Steam for 15 minutes or until they are
tender.

Arrange the asparagus on a serving dish and sprinkle
with grated cheese. Dribble over the melted butter and top
with poached eggs. Serve at once.

Valle d'Aosta   **BEETROOTS IN**   Serves 4
                       CREAM
                  Barbabietole alla crema

Save the beetroot tops for minestrone soup or a ravioli
filling; they are too rich in vitamins and minerals to throw
away.

675g (1½lb) beetroots
2 tablespoons olive oil
1 small onion, finely chopped
2 tablespoons fresh parsley, chopped
1 teaspoon fresh marjoram, or ¼ teaspoon dried
120ml (4floz) vegetable stock
1 teaspoon lemon juice
salt
freshly ground black pepper
50ml (2floz) single cream

Bake the beetroots in a moderate oven – 180°C (350°F/Gas Mark 4) – for 45 minutes to 1 hour, depending on their size, and slip off the skins. Cut into slices 5mm (¼ inch) thick.

Heat the olive oil in a frying pan and cook the onion, parsley and marjoram for 1 minute. Add the sliced beetroot and cook over a moderate heat for 2 minutes. Add the stock, lemon juice, salt and pepper, bring to the boil and simmer for 15 minutes until most of the liquid is evaporated. Stir in the cream and heat through. Serve at once.

Emilia-
Romagna
BEETROOTS PARMIGIANA
Serves 6
Barbabietole alla parmigiana

Alla parmigiana does not always mean that a dish comes from the town of Parma, but can indicate that the dish is sprinkled with Parmesan cheese. Sometimes vegetables *alla parmigiana* are baked in a white sauce topped with Parmesan cheese as in this recipe.

675g (1½lb) beetroots, trimmed and baked (see previous
*   recipe)*
600ml (1 pint) béchamel sauce (see page 57)
100g (4oz) freshly grated Parmesan cheese
25g (1oz) butter

Cut the beetroots into thin slices and arrange a layer in a

well-buttered, shallow baking dish. Cover with a little béchamel sauce and sprinkle with a little grated cheese. Repeat the layers until all the ingredients are used up. Finish with Parmesan cheese and dot with butter.

Bake in a preheated oven at 190°C (375°F/Gas Mark 5) for 20 to 25 minutes or until the top is nicely browned.

Tuscany   **RED HARICOT BEANS**   Serves 6
IN RED WINE
Fagioli borlotti al vino rosso

Tuscany is famous for its bean dishes. The beans in this recipe are simmered in wine and cloves and enriched with a *soffrito* of olive oil, garlic and rosemary. Towards the end of cooking the sauce is thickened with a little butter and flour. Serve this with a potato dish, such as the *Tortino di patate* on page 156, and a tossed green salad.

350g (12oz) dried red haricot beans
450ml (¾ pint) red wine
1 small onion, chopped
3 whole cloves
120ml (4floz) olive oil
900ml (1½ pints) water
3 cloves garlic, crushed
1 sprig of fresh rosemary, or ¼ teaspoon dried
25g (1oz) butter
1 tablespoon flour
salt
freshly ground black pepper

Soak the beans in water overnight and drain. Place the beans in a heavy saucepan with the red wine, onion, cloves, 2 tablespoons of olive oil and the water. Bring to the boil, cover and simmer for 1½ to 2 hours or until the beans are tender.

Half-way through the cooking time, heat the remaining olive oil in a small frying pan and cook the garlic and rosemary for 1 minute. Add to the beans, stir well and continue cooking. When the beans are tender, pour off and reserve the cooking liquid.

Heat the butter in a saucepan, stir in the flour and cook over a moderate heat for 1 minute. Slowly pour in the reserved cooking liquid, salt and black pepper and simmer for 5 minutes. And the drained beans, stir well and simmer for a further 5 minutes to heat through before serving.

Tuscany   **WHITE BEANS WITH**   Serves 6
TOMATO AND SAGE
Fagioli all'uccelletto

This is one of Tuscany's most famous bean dishes. *Fagioli all'uccelletto* literally means 'beans like birds', supposedly because the sage, onion, garlic and tomato makes the flavour of the beans resemble that of small game birds.

350g (12oz) dried white cannelini beans
50ml (2floz) olive oil
25g (1oz) butter
3 garlic cloves, crushed
10 fresh sage leaves, or ½ teaspoon dried
225g (8oz) canned plum tomatoes, forced through a sieve or
    puréed in a food processor
salt
freshly ground black pepper

Soak the beans in water overnight and drain. Place them in a saucepan and cover with water. Bring to the boil, cover, and simmer for 1½ to 2 hours or until tender. Drain.

Heat the olive oil and butter in a saucepan and cook the garlic and sage for 1 minute. Add the puréed tomatoes and cook over a moderate heat for 3 minutes. Add the drained beans, season with salt and black pepper to taste and simmer for a further 5 minutes.

Sardinia   **BEANS WITH FENNEL**   Serves 4
              AND CABBAGE
              Fagioli alla gallurese

This simple peasant stew comes from the north-east of
Sardinia.

250g (9oz) dried white haricot beans
50ml (2floz) olive oil
2 garlic cloves, crushed
1 onion, chopped
3 fennel bulbs
½ Savoy cabbage, shredded
225g (8oz) canned plum tomatoes, forced through a sieve or
*   puréed in a food processor*
salt
freshly ground black pepper

Soak the beans in water overnight and drain. Place them
in a saucepan and cover with water. Bring to the boil, cover
and simmer for 1½ to 2 hours or until they are tender.

Meanwhile, heat the olive oil in a large saucepan and
cook the garlic and onion over a moderate heat for 5
minutes. Remove the outer stalks and leaves from the
fennel and cut into 5cm (2 inch) strips. Add to the onion
together with the shredded cabbage. Cover and simmer for
10 minutes, stirring occasionally. Add the puréed tomatoes, cover and simmer for 30 minutes or until the fennel
and cabbage are tender and the sauce is thickened.

When the beans are cooked, pour off and reserve 250ml
(8floz) of the cooking liquid. Add the beans and cooking
liquid to the fennel and cabbage with salt and pepper to
taste and simmer together for 5 minutes.

Piedmont   **'RATATOUILLE'**   Serves 6
OF FRENCH BEANS
Fagiolini in umido

This is a speciality of Domodossola.

900g (2lb) French beans
2 tablespoons olive oil
1 small onion, chopped
2 garlic cloves, crushed
2 tablespoons fresh parsley, finely chopped
1 teaspoon fresh basil, or ¼ teaspoon dried
50ml (2fl oz) dry red wine
225g (8oz) canned plum tomatoes and their juice, seeded
   and chopped
salt
freshly ground black pepper

Top and tail the beans and cut them into 5cm (2 inch) lengths. Heat the olive oil in a large frying pan and cook the onion, garlic, parsley and basil for 3 minutes. Add the red wine and cook over a moderate heat until the wine is almost evaporated. Add the beans and the tomatoes, season to taste with salt and black pepper and cook gently for 30 minutes or until the beans are tender and the sauce is thickened.

Sicily   **BROCCOLI SIMMERED**   Serves 6
WITH LEEKS
AND WHITE WINE
Broccoli affogati

900g (2lb) broccoli
2 leeks, white part only
3 tablespoons olive oil
2 garlic cloves, crushed
2 tablespoons parsley, finely chopped
50ml (2fl oz) dry red wine
salt
freshly ground black pepper

Break the broccoli into florets and cut the stalks into 1 cm (½ inch) dice.

Trim away the roots of the leeks. Cut in half lengthwise and carefully wash away any dirt between the leaves. Cut into slices 1 cm (½ inch) thick.

Heat the olive oil in a large frying pan and cook the garlic and parsley for 1 minute. Add the leeks and cook over moderate heat for 5 minutes, stirring occasionally so the leeks cook evenly. Add the broccoli and dry white wine and season with salt and black pepper to taste. Bring to the boil and simmer, covered, for 10 minutes or until the broccoli is tender and the wine is evaporated.

| Emilia-Romagna | **BRUSSELS SPROUTS PARMIGIANA** | Serves 6 |

Cavolini di bruxelles alla parmigiana

The Brussels sprouts are steamed and briefly cooked in butter then dressed with Parmesan cheese, which gives them a delicious 'nutty' flavour. Take care not to overcook them.

675g (1½lb) Brussels sprouts
50g (2oz) butter
75g (3oz) freshly grated Parmesan cheese
salt
freshly ground black pepper

Trim the root ends of the Brussels sprouts and remove any yellowish leaves. Steam for 8 to 10 minutes or until they are just tender.

Heat the butter in a large frying pan. Add the Brussels sprouts and stir well to coat them evenly in butter. Sprinkle with Parmesan cheese and season with salt and black pepper to taste. Stir again and serve at once.

All Italy   **SWEET AND**   Serves 6
                      SOUR CABBAGE
                      WITH CAPERS
                      Cavalo in agrodolce

This winter vegetable dish is found in many regions of Italy.

2 tablespoons olive oil
1 small onion, chopped
1 green cabbage, shredded
2 tablespoons hot water
225g (8oz) canned plum tomatoes, forced through a sieve or
*   puréed in a food processor*
2 tablespoons wine vinegar
1 tablespoon capers
2 teaspoons sugar or honey
salt
freshly ground black pepper

Heat the olive oil in a large saucepan and cook the onion over a moderate heat for 3 minutes. Add the shredded cabbage and hot water and simmer, covered, for 10 minutes, stirring occasionally so the cabbage cooks evenly.

Add the puréed tomatoes, vinegar, capers, sugar, salt and black pepper to taste and stir well. Cover and simmer for 30 minutes or until the cabbage is very tender and the sauce is reduced.

Liguria   **CARROT FRICASSEE**   Serves 6
Carote in fricassea

40g (1½oz) butter
2 tablespoons parsley, finely chopped
675g (1½lb) carrots, diced
3 tablespoons hot water
2 egg yolks
120ml (4floz) double cream
salt
freshly ground black pepper

Heat the butter in a saucepan and cook the parsley and carrots for 3 minutes. Add the hot water, cover and simmer for 20 minutes or until the carrots are tender and the liquid has evaporated.

Beat the egg yolks and cream together and pour over the carrots. Cook over a moderate heat until the sauce is slightly thickened; do not boil. Season with salt and black pepper to taste. Serve at once.

Tuscany   **CAULIFLOWER AND**   Serves 6
POTATO PIE
Pasticcio do cavolfiore e patate

1 small cauliflower (about 675g) (1½lb))
675g (1½lb) potatoes, peeled
75g (3oz) butter
50ml (2floz) double cream
⅛ teaspoon freshly grated nutmeg
salt
freshly ground black pepper
3 tablespoons wholemeal breadcrumbs or wheatgerm

Break the cauliflower into florets and steam them for 10 minutes or until tender. Bring the potatoes to the boil in lightly salted water and cook for 20 minutes or until they are tender. Force the cauliflower and potatoes through a sieve. Add half the butter, the cream and nutmeg with salt and black pepper to taste and mix well.

Grease a baking dish and sprinkle with breadcrumbs or wheatgerm. Turn the dish over and shake out any excess. Spoon in the cauliflower and potato mixture. Melt the remaining butter in a small pan and dribble over the top. Bake in a preheated oven at 200°C (400°F/Gas Mark 6) for 20 minutes or until the top is golden.

Lombardy   **CELERY GRATIN**   Serves 4
Sedani gratinati

This is a speciality of Verona.

2 heads celery
2 tablespoons olive oil
600 ml (1 pint) béchamel sauce (see page 57)
50 g (2 oz) grated Gruyère cheese
⅛ teaspoon freshly grated nutmeg
salt
freshly ground black pepper
2 tablespoons freshly grated Parmesan cheese
2 tablespoons wholemeal breadcrumbs or wheatgerm
25 g (1 oz) butter

Remove the root ends and the leaves of the celery. Cut the stalks into 5 cm (2 inch) lengths and steam for 10 minutes or until they are tender. Heat the olive oil in a large frying pan and cook the celery over a moderate heat until it is golden on both sides.

Prepare the béchamel sauce, remove from the heat and stir in the Gruyère cheese and nutmeg with salt and black pepper to taste. Spoon some of the sauce into the bottom of a large, shallow baking dish. Arrange the celery on top, then pour over the remaining sauce. Combine the Parmesan cheese with the breadcrumbs or wheatgerm and sprinkle over the top. Dot with butter and bake in a preheated oven at 200°C (400°F/Gas Mark 6) for 20 minutes or until the top is golden.

Veneto   **COURGETTES,**   Serves 6
            VENETIAN STYLE
            Zucchine alla veneta

900g (2 lb) courgettes
25g (1 oz) butter
3 tablespoons olive oil
2 tablespoons parsley, finely chopped
2 eggs plus 1 egg yolk
25g (1 oz) freshly grated Parmesan cheese
salt
freshly ground black pepper

Trim the ends of the courgettes and cut into rounds 3 mm (⅛ inch) thick. Heat the butter and olive oil in a large frying pan and cook the courgettes and parsley over a moderately high heat until they are golden on both sides.

Beat together the eggs, egg yolk and Parmesan cheese. Season with salt and black pepper to taste and pour over the courgettes. Cook, stirring constantly, for 1 or 2 minutes or until the courgettes are evenly coated. Serve at once.

Liguria   **AUBERGINE AND**   Serves 4
           TOMATO GRATIN   to 6
        Melanzane e pomodoro gratinati

This is one of my favourite baked vegetable dishes and has a wonderful 'Mediterranean flavour'.

3 medium aubergines (about 900g (2 lb))
salt
about 175 ml (6 fl oz) olive oil
2 garlic cloves, crushed
a handful of parsley, chopped
900g (2 lb) ripe plum tomatoes, peeled, seeded and chopped
freshly ground black pepper
50g (2 oz) wholemeal breadcrumbs
2 tablespoons freshly grated Parmesan cheese

Peel the aubergines and cut them into slices 3 mm (⅛ inch) thick. Sprinkle with salt and set in a colander for 1 hour to release the bitter juices. Wash off the salt and pat dry. Fry the slices in 2 tablespoons of hot oil until golden on both sides. Drain on a paper towel.

Heat 2 tablespoons olive oil in a large frying pan and cook the garlic and parsley for 1 minute. Add the tomatoes and cook over a moderate heat for 15 minutes. Season with salt and black pepper.

Place a layer of aubergine slices on the bottom of a shallow baking dish. Spread a little of the cooked tomatoes over the top and sprinkle lightly with breadcrumbs. Repeat the layers until all the ingredients are used up, ending with breadcrumbs. Sprinkle the top with Parmesan cheese and dribble 2 tablespoons olive oil over the top. Bake in a preheated oven at 180°C (350°F/Gas Mark 4) for 30 to 35 minutes or until the top is golden.

Campania and
the South

GRILLED AUBERGINE SLICES

Serves 4
to 6

Melanzane alla griglia

2 medium aubergines (about 550g (1¼lb))
about 120ml (4floz) olive oil
350ml (12fl oz) tomato sauce (see page 54)
175g (6oz) freshly grated Parmesan cheese

Trim the ends of the aubergines but do not peel them. Cut into slices 1cm (½ inch) thick. Arrange in one layer on a well-greased baking sheet and brush each slice liberally with olive oil. Cover with foil and bake in a preheated oven at 200°C (400°F/Gas Mark 6) for 15 minutes or until the aubergine is tender but not mushy.

Remove the foil and spread a little tomato sauce over the aubergine slices. Sprinkle them with Parmesan cheese. Place under a preheated hot grill for a few minutes until the top is golden.

Liguria   **AUBERGINE AND**   Serves 6
           COURGETTES SIMMERED
           WITH MUSHROOMS
                Funghetto

Funghetto means 'cooked like mushrooms' or cooked in
olive oil, garlic and herbs.

120 ml (4 fl oz) olive oil
2 garlic cloves, crushed
a handful of parsley, finely chopped
1 tablespoon fresh oregano, or ½ teaspoon dried
2 small aubergines, not peeled, cut into 1 cm (½ inch)
   cubes
2 small courgettes, sliced
100 g (4 oz) mushrooms, sliced
salt
freshly ground black pepper

Heat the olive oil in a large frying pan and cook the garlic,
parsley and oregano for 1 minute. Add the aubergines,
courgettes and mushrooms and cook, covered, over a
moderate heat for 10 minutes or until the vegetables are
tender and turning golden. Season with salt and black
pepper. Simmer for another 2 minutes.

Campania   **AUBERGINES SIMMERED**   Serves 4
            WITH TOMATOES
               AND HERBS
           Melanzane al funghetto

Fresh plum tomatoes are best for this recipe. If they are
unavailable, canned plum tomatoes can be used but take
care to drain off any juice before adding them to the
aubergines.

2 medium aubergines (about 550 g (1¼ lb))
about 175 ml (6 fl oz) olive oil
2 garlic cloves, crushed
1 tablespoon fresh basil, or ¼ teaspoon dried

1 tablespoon parsley, finely chopped
1 tablespoon fresh oregano, or ¼ teaspoon dried
6 ripe plum tomatoes, peeled, seeded and cut into strips
salt
freshly ground black pepper

Trim the ends of the aubergines but do not peel them. Cut into 1 cm (½ inch) cubes.

Heat the oil in a large frying pan and cook the garlic, basil, parsley and oregano for 1 minute. Add the aubergine cubes, cover and simmer for 30 minutes, stirring occasionally until the aubergine is tender. Add the tomatoes, with salt and black pepper to taste. Cover and simmer for a further 10 minutes.

Emilia-Romagna **FENNEL GRATIN**   Serves 6
and the North   *Finocchii gratinati*

6 fennel bulbs
450 ml (¾ pint) béchamel sauce (see page 57)
3 tablespoons single cream
2 tablespoons freshly grated Parmesan cheese
15 g (½ oz) wholemeal breadcrumbs or wheatgerm
25 g (1 oz) butter

Remove the outer stalks and leaves from the fennel bulbs. Trim the bases and cut into wedges. Steam the fennel for 30 to 40 minutes until the pieces are just tender.

Prepare the béchamel sauce and stir in the single cream. Spoon a little in the bottom of a shallow baking dish. Arrange the fennel on top in one layer and pour over the remaining sauce. Combine the Parmesan cheese and the breadcrumbs or wheatgerm and sprinkle over the top. Dot with butter and bake in a preheated oven at 200°C (400°F/Gas Mark 6) for 20 minutes or until the top is golden.

Campania   **FENNEL SIMMERED**   Serves 4
                 WITH ONION
                 AND TOMATO
                 Finocchio al pomodoro

If fresh plum tomatoes are unavailable, canned plum tomatoes can be used instead.

2 fennel bulbs, about 450g (1 lb)
2 tablespoons olive oil
2 garlic cloves, crushed
1 medium onion, thinly sliced
2 tablespoons fresh parsley, finely chopped
400g (1 lb) ripe plum tomatoes, peeled, seeded and chopped
salt
freshly ground black pepper

Remove the outer stalks and leaves from the fennel bulbs. Trim the bases and cut into thin wedges.

Heat the olive oil in a large frying pan and cook the garlic, onion and parsley for 3 minutes. Add the fennel and cook for another 2 minutes, stirring well, so the fennel is well coated with oil. Add the tomatoes and season to taste with salt and black pepper. Cover, and simmer for 20 to 30 minutes, or until the fennel is just tender. Serve hot.

Calabria   **GIANFOTTERE**   Serves 4
                Gianfottere

This is a delicious combination, similar to the French *ratatouille* but with the addition of potatoes and a pinch of saffron.

225g (8oz) potatoes, peeled
225g (8oz) courgettes
2 red peppers
1 medium aubergine, about 225g (8oz)
about 120ml (4floz) olive oil
1 large onion, thinly sliced
2 tablespoons fresh parsley, chopped
2 tablespoons fresh basil or ½ teaspoon dried
1 tablespoon fresh oregano or ½ teaspoon dried
a pinch of powdered saffron
225g (8oz) plum tomatoes, peeled, seeded and coarsely
   chopped
salt
freshly ground black pepper

Bring the potatoes to the boil in lightly salted water and cook for 20 minutes, or until they are just tender. Drain and cut into fairly thick slices.

Trim the courgettes and cut them into rounds 3mm (⅛ inch) thick. Remove the pith and core from the peppers and cut them into strips. Peel the aubergines and cut into slices about the same thickness as the courgettes.

Heat 2 tablespoons of olive oil in a large heavy frying pan and cook the courgettes over a moderately high heat until they are golden on both sides. Set aside and drain off any excess oil back into the frying pan. Repeat with the peppers and the aubergines, adding more oil as necessary.

Heat the remaining olive oil in the same frying pan and cook the onion, herbs and saffron over moderate heat for 5 minutes, or until the onions are translucent. Add the chopped tomatoes and continue to cook for a further 5 minutes. Stir in the courgettes, peppers, aubergine and potatoes, and season with salt and black pepper to taste.

Cover and simmer for 5 more minutes to blend the flavours. Serve at once.

| Apulia | **LEEKS BRAISED WITH CARROTS AND TOMATOES** | Serves 4 to 6 |

Porri in stufato

This is a particularly light and delicious combination.

6 leeks
3 tablespoons olive oil
2 small carrots, diced
6 ripe plum tomatoes, peeled, seeded and chopped
salt
freshly ground black pepper

Trim away the root ends of the leeks. Cut in half lengthwise and carefully wash away any dirt between the leaves. Cut into 5cm (2 inch) lengths; use the whole leek, including the dark green parts.

Heat the olive oil in a large saucepan and cook the leeks and carrots, covered, over a moderate heat for 5 minutes. Add the tomatoes, cover and simmer for 30 minutes, or until the carrots are tender. Season with salt and pepper to taste and serve hot.

| Lombardy | **LENTIL PURÉE WITH CREAM** | Serves 6 |

Purea di lenticchie

350g (12oz) green lentils
1 bay leaf
2 tablespoons olive oil
1 garlic clove, crushed
1 onion, finely chopped
1 stalk celery, thinly sliced
2 tablespoons fresh parsley, finely chopped
a pinch of ground cloves
salt

freshly ground black pepper
25 g (1 oz) butter
50 ml (2 fl oz) double cream

Soak the lentils in water overnight and drain. Place in a saucepan with the bay leaf, cover with water and bring to the boil. Cover and simmer for 1½ hours or until the lentils are soft. Remove the bay leaf.

Heat the olive oil in another saucepan and cook the garlic, onion, celery and parsley over a moderate heat for 5 minutes. Add to the lentils, together with the cloves and salt and black pepper to taste. If necessary, increase the heat slightly to reduce the cooking liquid. Cook for a further 15 minutes.

Force the lentils through a sieve or purée in a blender. Return to the pan. Stir in the butter and the cream and simmer for a further 5 minutes. Serve at once.

Liguria **MUSHROOMS WITH** Serves 4
PINE NUTS to 6
Funghi trifolati con pignoli

2 tablespoons olive oil
1 garlic clove, crushed
1 small onion, finely chopped
1 tablespoon fresh parsley, chopped
1 tablespoon fresh marjoram, or ¼ teaspoon dried
675 g (1½ lb) mushrooms, sliced
50 g (2 oz) pine nuts
salt
freshly ground black pepper

Heat the olive oil in a frying pan and cook the garlic, onion, parsley and marjoram over a moderate heat for 3 minutes. Add the mushrooms and pine nuts and stir well. Cook over a moderate heat for 5 minutes or until the mushrooms are slightly browned. Season with salt and black pepper to taste and serve immediately.

Piedmont **BRAISED ONIONS** Serves 6
AND PEAS
Cipolle e piselli in umido

2 tablespoons olive oil
1 garlic clove, crushed
2 tablespoons fresh parsley, finely chopped
450g (1lb) small pickling onions, peeled
350g (12oz) shelled fresh peas
120ml (4floz) hot vegetable stock
salt
freshly ground black pepper
2 tablespoons double cream

Heat the olive oil in a saucepan and cook the garlic and
parsley for 1 minute. Add the onions, peas and stock.
Cover and simmer for 20 to 25 minutes or until the peas
are tender and the liquid has evaporated. Season to taste
with salt and black pepper. Stir in the cream. Heat
through and serve at once.

Valle d'Aosta **SPLIT PEA CREAM** Serves 4
Purea di piselli

175g (6oz) split peas
2 tablespoons olive oil
1 leek, thinly sliced
1/4 Webb's lettuce, shredded
900ml (1 1/2 pints) vegetable stock or water
40g (1 1/2oz) butter
salt
freshly ground black pepper

Soak the split peas in water overnight and drain. Heat the
olive oil in a saucepan and cook the leek over a moderate
heat for 8 minutes or until it is tender, stirring from time to
time so the leek cooks evenly.
　Add the lettuce, split peas and stock and bring to the
boil. Cover and simmer for 1 1/4 to 1 1/2 hours or until the
split peas are tender. Force through a sieve or purée in a

blender. Return to the pan and add the butter and salt and black pepper to taste. Simmer for 5 minutes.

Abruzzi　　**GOLDEN FRIED PEPPERS**　　Serves 6
Peperoni dorati

The Italians love deep fried vegetables. This dish is very simple to prepare: the peppers are cut into strips, dipped in flour then beaten egg, and deep fried until crisp and golden. Sometimes a little grated Parmesan cheese is added to enhance the flavour. Courgettes, aubergines, mushrooms and onions all make suitable variations.

6 green peppers
wholemeal flour for dusting
2 eggs, beaten
oil for deep frying
6 lemon wedges

Grill the peppers until they are blackened all over. Wash under cold water and remove the skins. Cut into strips about 2.5 cm (1 inch) wide. Dip in flour then beaten egg and fry in hot oil until golden on both sides. Drain on a paper towel and serve at once with lemon wedges on the side.

Liguria　　**POTATOES WITH**　　Serves
　　　　　　WALNUTS　　4 to 6
Patate alla provinciale

This is exotic and full of flavour.

900 g (2 lb) waxy potatoes
4 tablespoons olive oil
25 g (1 oz) butter
2 garlic cloves, crushed
1 teaspoon fresh chopped basil, or ¼ teaspoon dried
1 tablespoon of fresh parsley, finely chopped
1 small onion, finely chopped

grated rind of 1 lemon
salt
freshly ground black pepper
juice of ½ lemon
25g (1oz) walnuts, ground in a blender

Peel the potatoes and bring to boil in lightly salted water. Cook for 20 minutes or until the potatoes are just tender. Drain and cut into slices. Heat the olive oil in a large frying pan and cook the garlic, basil, parsley, onion and lemon rind for 2 minutes. Add the potatoes and salt and black pepper to taste. Cook over moderate heat for 10 minutes or until they are golden on both sides. Sprinkle with lemon juice and ground walnuts. Toss lightly and serve.

Campania **POTATOES WITH** Serves 4 to 6
TOMATOES
Patate alla pizzaiola

675g (1½lb) potatoes
2 garlic cloves, crushed
3 tablespoons olive oil
6 ripe plum tomatoes, peeled, seeded and chopped
1 tablespoon fresh basil, or ½ teaspoon dried
salt
freshly ground black pepper

Bring the potatoes to boil in lightly salted water and cook for 20 minutes or until the potatoes are tender. Drain and cut into slices.

Heat the olive oil in a large frying pan and cook the garlic for 1 minute. Add the chopped tomatoes and cook over moderate heat for 8 minutes. Add the potatoes and basil and season with salt and black pepper to taste. Simmer for 5 minutes to blend the flavours.

Lazio   **TURNIP TOPS WITH**   Serves 6
            GARLIC AND OIL
         Broccoletti con aglio e olio

The Roman way of cooking greens in garlic and oil is very
simple and delicious. Swiss chard, beet leaves, spinach,
kale, sprouting broccoli and spring greens can all be cooked
the same way.

3 tablespoons olive oil
3 garlic cloves, crushed
900g (2lb) turnip tops, cut into 7.5cm (3 inch) lengths
3 tablespoons hot water
salt
freshly ground black pepper

Heat the olive oil in a large saucepan and cook the garlic
for 1 minute. Add the turnip tops, hot water, salt and
pepper. Cook, covered, for 8 to 10 minutes or until tender,
stirring occasionally so the greens cook evenly.

DESSERTS

DOLCI

Italians usually end their meals with fresh fruit, with or without some cheese. Cakes and pastries are usually bought in pastry shops, or eaten in the middle of the afternoon with a cup of coffee.

In this chapter I have included a selection of cakes and fruit desserts that can be quickly and easily made at home, plus a few traditional custards and creams that are suited to family meals and informal entertaining.

Many of the recipes I have chosen are traditionally sweetened with honey. In most cases, either honey or sugar may be used according to your preference.

Veneto	**PUMPKIN CAKE** *Torta di zucca*	Serves 12 to 16

This is a moist cake with a delicious flavour.

225g (7oz) wholemeal flour

1½ teaspoons baking powder
2 teaspoons bicarbonate of soda
¼ teaspoon salt
1 teaspoon cinnamon
¼ teaspoon freshly grated nutmeg
250g (9oz) cooked pumpkin, forced through a sieve or
    puréed in a food processor
100g (4floz) bland oil (soya or peanut oil are best)
125g (5floz) clear honey
2 tablespoons rum
2 eggs
grated rind of 1 lemon
50g (2oz) raisins

Butter a 23–25cm (9–10 inch) diameter, spring-sided cake tin and dust with flour. Combine the flours, baking powder, bicarbonate of soda, salt, cinnamon and nutmeg in a bowl and set aside.

Beat the pumpkin purée with the oil in a large mixing bowl. Gradually stir in the honey and the rum. Beat the eggs well and add a little at a time to the mixture, blending well after each addition. Fold in the dry ingredients, mixing well. Lastly, stir in the grated lemon rind and the raisins.

Turn into the prepared tin. Bake in the lower third of a preheated oven at 180°C (350°F/Gas Mark 4) for 45 to 50 minutes or until a knife comes out clean from the centre of the cake.

Let the cake cool for 10 minutes in the tin, then gently invert on to a cake rack to cool completely.

Tuscany **ALMOND SPONGE CAKE** Serves 6
Bocca di dama to 8

Bocca di dama literally means 'Milady's mouth', probably
to point out that this cake is fine enough for an aristocrat.

15g (¹/₂oz) butter
flour for dusting
6 eggs, separated
100g (4oz) sugar
50g (2oz) unblanched almonds, finely ground in a blender
100g (4oz) wholemeal flour
grated rind of 1 lemon

Butter a 23–25cm (9–10 inch) diameter, spring-sided
cake tin and dust with flour.

Beat the egg yolks with the sugar until very light. Add
the ground almonds, flour and lemon rind and blend well
together. Beat the egg whites stiff and carefully fold into
the mixture. Pour into the prepared tin. Bake for 40
minutes in a preheated oven at 160°C (325°F/Gas Mark 3)
or until a knife comes out clean from the centre of the cake.

Ligiura **CORNMEAL APPLE CAKE** Serves 6
Torta di mele

This is a simple rustic dessert. Use the coarse cornmeal
found in Italian groceries.

65g (2¹/₂oz) wholemeal flour
50g (2oz) cornmeal
2 teaspoons baking powder
¹/₂ teaspoon salt
¹/₄ teaspoon freshly grated nutmeg
¹/₄ teaspoon mace
5 or 6 apples
2 tablespoons lemon juice
¹/₂ teaspoon ground cinnamon
2 eggs
175ml (6floz) milk

100g (4oz) sugar
65g (2½oz) butter, melted

Butter a 23-25cm (9-10 inch) diameter, ceramic or glass flan dish and dust with flour. Combine the flour, cornmeal, baking powder, salt, nutmeg and mace in a large bowl and set aside. Peel, quarter and slice the apples and sprinkle with lemon juice and cinnamon.

Beat the eggs lightly and add the milk, sugar and melted butter. Stir into the flour mixture to make a thin batter. Fold in the apples and pour into the prepared tin. Bake in a preheated oven at 180°C (350°F/Gas Mark 4) for 35 to 40 minutes or until the top is golden. Serve warm or cold.

| Trentino, | **CARROT ALMOND TORTE** | Serves 6 |
| Alto Adige | *Torta di carote* | to 8 |

225g (8oz) finely grated carrots
250g (9 oz) unblanched almonds, finely ground in a blender
25g (1oz) wholemeal breadcrumbs
2 teaspoons baking powder
4 eggs separated
100g (4oz) sugar
grated rind of 1 lemon

Butter a 23cm (9 inch) diameter, spring-sided cake tin and dust with flour. Combine the carrots, ground almonds, breadcrumbs and baking powder in a large bowl and set aside.

Beat the egg yolks and sugar until light and add to the carrot mixture with the lemon rind, blending well. Beat the egg whites until stiff and fold into the mixture. Pour into the prepared tin and bake for 50 to 60 minutes in a preheated oven at 180°C (350°F/Gas Mark 3) or until a knife comes out clean from the centre of the cake.

Lazio **ROMAN CHEESECAKE** Serves 6
Torta di ricotta

Italian cheesecakes are less rich than American cheese-cakes. Crystallized fruits are usually included in this recipe, but I prefer to use dried apricots instead.

15g (½oz) butter
flour for dusting
350g (12oz) Ricotta cheese
2 tablespoons of flour
4 tablespoons sugar or honey
3 eggs, separated
40g (1½oz) raisins
2 tablespoons dried apricots, cut into very small dice
2 tablespoons rum or dry Marsala
grated rind of 1 lemon

Butter a 18cm (7 inch) round cake tin 9cm (3½ inch) deep and dust it with flour. Combine the Ricotta cheese, flour, sugar and egg yolks in a large bowl and blend well. Stir in dried apricots, rum and lemon rind. Beat the egg whites until stiff and fold into the mixture.

Pour into the prepared tin. Bake in a preheated oven at 180°C (350°F/Gas Mark 4) for 40 to 50 minutes or until the top is golden and a knife comes out clean from the centre of the cake.

Alto Adige **APPLE STRUDEL** Serves 6
Apfelstrudel

The Austrian influence is still very strong in the Alto Adige which is reflected in many of the delicious pastries and strudels that are made in the region. It is easy to make perfect apple strudel with commercial strudel dough or filo pastry. Be sure to allow at least 2 hours for the pastry to thaw out and be ready for use.

4 large cooking apples
3 sheets filo pastry (30 × 40cm (12 × 16 inches)), thawed

about 65 ml (2½ fl oz) olive oil
50 g (2 oz) raisins
50 g (2 oz) shelled almonds, finely ground in a blender
2 tablespoons pine nuts
50 g (2 oz) wheatgerm
grated rind of 1 lemon
1 teaspoon ground cinnamon
4 tablespoons sugar and honey
25 g (1 oz) butter, melted.

Peel, core and slice the apples thinly.

Cover the table or working top with a clean cloth. Lay a sheet of filo pastry on the cloth and brush lightly with oil. Place another sheet of pastry on top and repeat until all five sheets have been brushed with oil. Arrange the apples over the third of the pastry nearest to you. Sprinkle with raisins, ground almonds, pine nuts, wheatgerm and lemon rind. Sprinkle with cinnamon and dribble the honey and then the melted butter over the top. Carefully pick up the corners of the cloth closest to you and gently lift the cloth and let the strudel roll over once. Brush the top lightly with oil and then lift the cloth again and let the strudel roll over completely. Brush the top lightly with oil.

Pick up the cloth and the strudel and very carefully twist on to a greased baking sheet. Brush the top with oil. Bake in the lower third of a preheated oven at 180°C (350°F/Gas Mark 4) for 35 to 40 minutes or until the apples are just tender and the pastry is crisp and golden. Allow to cool before serving.

Lombardy   **APPLE CHARLOTTE**   Serves 6
FLAMBÉE
Ciarlotta di mele

900 g (2 lb) apples
100 g (4 oz) butter
5 tablespoons honey or sugar, or to taste
75 g (3 oz) raisins
25 g (1 oz) pine nuts

grated rind of 1 lemon
7 or 8 slices of bread
about 175 ml (6 fl oz) rum

Peel, core and slice the apples. Heat 25 g (1 oz) butter in a
heavy saucepan and add the apples and honey. Simmer
until the mixture has the consistency of a thick purée.
Remove from the heat and add the raisins, pine nuts and
lemon rind.

Butter a charlotte mould or a deep cake tin. Melt the
rest of the butter, dip in the bread and line the bottom and
sides of the mould tightly with bread slices. Fill with the
apple mixture, top with the remaining slices of bread and
brush the top with melted butter.

Bake in a preheated oven at 180°C (350°F/Gas Mark 4)
for 35 to 40 minutes or until the top is golden. Carefully
turn out on to a serving dish. Pour the heated rum over the
charlotte and set alight.

Keep the apple filling thick. If it is too liquid, it would
soften the bread and the charlotte would collapse.

Lombardy **PEAR AND ALMOND** Serves 4
and the **PUDDING** to 6
North *Torta di pere e mandorle*

This simple rustic dessert is a favourite with children.
Apples can be used instead of pears.

50 g (2 oz) wholemeal breadcrumbs
6 pears
50 g (2 oz) ground almonds
50 g (2 oz) raisins
50 g (2 oz) sugar
grated rind of 1 lemon
40 g (1½ oz) butter
65 ml (2½ fl oz) water

Butter a baking dish and sprinkle the bottom and sides
with breadcrumbs. Peel, core and slice the pears and place
a layer over the bottom of the baking dish. Sprinkle with

ground almonds, raisins, sugar and grated lemon rind. Sprinkle with more breadcrumbs and dot with butter. Repeat the layers until all the ingredients are used, ending with breadcrumbs and butter. Pour in the water.

Bake in a preheated oven at 180°C (350°F/Gas Mark 4) for 30 to 40 minutes or until the pears are tender and the top is golden.

Veneto
CORNMEAL COOKIES WITH RAISINS AND PINE NUTS
Zaletti

Makes about 36 cookies

Zaletti are traditional Venetian raisin cookies made with a mixture of cornmeal and wholemeal flour and flavoured with lemon rind, vanilla and pine nuts. *Zaletti* means yellow.

75g (3oz) raisins
50ml (2floz) brandy
200g (7oz) wholemeal flour
100g (4oz) cornmeal
¼ teaspoon salt
3 egg yolks
150g (5oz) clear honey
100g (4oz) butter, melted
40g (1½oz) pine nuts
grated rind of 1 lemon
½ teaspoon vanilla essence

Place the raisins in a small bowl and pour the brandy over them. Allow to steep for 1 to 2 hours. Combine the flour, cornmeal and salt in a large bowl and set aside.

Beat the egg yolks with the honey until light and creamy. Add to the flour and cornmeal mixture together with the melted butter, the raisins soaked in brandy, pine nuts, lemon rind and vanilla. Mix to a soft dough. Roll out to 3mm (⅛ inch) thick and cut into diamond shapes and arrange on a well-buttered baking sheet. Bake in a preheated oven at 190°C (375°F/Gas Mark 5) oven for 10 to 15 minutes or until the cookies are turning golden.

Lombardy   **APPLE FRITTERS**   Serves 4
                Laciadett de pomm   to 6

A speciality of Brianza.

250g (9oz) wholemeal or plain white flour
½ teaspoon salt
2 eggs, separated
65ml (2½floz) rum
250ml (8floz) water
4 to 5 apples
oil for deep frying
sugar or honey
1 lemon, cut into wedges

Combine the flour and salt in a bowl and make a well in the centre. Add the egg yolks, 1 tablespoon rum and half the water. Blend well together. Gradually stir in the remaining water until the batter is smooth. Allow to stand for 1 hour.

Peel and core the apples and cut into rounds 3mm (⅛ inch) thick. Place in a shallow bowl and pour the remaining rum over them. Allow the apples to steep for 30 minutes.

Beat the egg whites until stiff and fold into the batter. Dip the apple rings into the batter and fry in hot oil until golden on both sides. Drain on a paper towel, dust with sugar and serve at once with lemon wedges on the side.

Sicily   **ORANGES AND CURAÇAO**   Serves 6
              Arance e curaçao

This is light and refreshing.

6 large oranges
175ml (6floz) Curaçao
2 tablespoons clear honey, warmed

Peel the oranges and remove all the white pith. Cut into slices 3mm (¼ inch) thick and place in a glass serving dish. Mix the Curaçao with the warmed honey until it is dissolved and pour over the orange slices. Chill thoroughly before serving.

Lazio **STRAWBERRIES WITH ORANGE JUICE** Serves 4 to 6
Fragole al arancia

675g (1½lb) strawberries
2 tablespoons clear honey, warmed
juice of 2 oranges
1 tablespoon Curaçao

Wash and hull the strawberries and place in individual glass dishes. Stir the warmed honey into the orange juice until it is dissolved. Add the Curaçao and pour over the strawberries. Chill thoroughly before serving.

Piedmont   **STRAWBERRIES WITH**   Serves 6
RICOTTA CREAM
Ricotta con le fragole

Ricotta cheese is used a great deal in Italian desserts. In this recipe the Ricotta is mixed with egg yolks, milk, cream and a dash of liqueur. This makes a wonderful alternative to whipped cream.

675 g (1½ lb) strawberries
450 g (1 lb) Ricotta cheese
2 egg yolks
2 tablespoons rum
grated rind of 1 lemon
3 tablespoons honey or sugar
50 ml (2 fl oz) double cream, whipped

Wash and hull the strawberries and place in individual glass dishes. Force the Ricotta cheese through a fine sieve into a mixing bowl. Add the egg yolks, rum, lemon rind and honey and blend well together. Fold in the whipped cream and spoon the mixture over the strawberries. Chill thoroughly before serving.

All Italy   **BAKED APPLES WITH**   Serves 6
HONEY, RAISINS AND
MARSALA
Mele al forno

6 large cooking apples
75 g (3 oz) raisins
2 tablespoons pine nuts
grated rind of 1 lemon
6 tablespoons honey
50 ml (2 fl oz) sweet Marsala
120 ml (4 fl oz) water

Wash and core the apples but do not peel them. Arrange them in a shallow baking dish. Spoon some of the raisins, pine nuts, lemon rind and honey into each apple. Pour a little Marsala over the top.

Pour the water into the bottom of the baking dish. Bake in a preheated oven at 180°C (350°F/Gas Mark 4) for 45 minutes to 1 hour or until the apples are tender. Baste once or twice during cooking.

| Piedmont | **CHERRIES IN BAROLO WINE** *Ciliege in barolo* | Serves 4 to 6 |

Fruit compôtes are served all over Italy. This is a classic Piedmontese compôte that is cooked in spiced red wine. Plums, pears, apples and peaches can all be cooked in the same way. Any good dry red wine may be used instead of Barolo wine.

675g (1½lb) cherries
3 tablespoons honey or sugar
450ml (¾ pint) Barolo wine
½ cinnamon stick
2 strips orange rind

Wash and stem the cherries, then remove the stones. Place the cherries in a saucepan with the honey, red wine, cinnamon stick and orange rind. Bring to the boil and simmer for 10 minutes. Pour into a glass serving dish and chill thoroughly in a refrigerator. Remove the cinnamon to serve.

| Sicily | **PEARS WITH ZABAGLIONE** *Pere allo zabaglione* | Serves 6 |

Zabaglione is one of Italy's most famous desserts. It is a delectable frothy cream made with egg yolks, sugar and wine, usually Marsala. Sometimes gelatine or whipped cream is added, and if it is frozen, this dessert is transformed into a marvellous *semi freddo* or half-frozen ice cream.

Fruit Compôte
6 pears
250 ml (8 fl oz) water
2 or 3 tablespoons sugar or honey

Zabaglione cream
2 egg yolks
3 tablespoons sugar
50 ml (2 fl oz) sweet Marsala
120 ml (4 fl oz) double cream, whipped
½ teaspoon vanilla essence

Peel the pears and cut them in half lengthwise. Remove the core. Bring the water and sugar to the boil in a saucepan and poach the pears for 5 minutes or until they are just tender. Place the pears in individual glass bowls and chill in the refrigerator.

To make the zabaglione, whisk the egg yolks and 2 tablespoons sugar together in the top of a double saucepan over hot, not boiling, water. Gradually add the Marsala, beating constantly until the mixture starts to thicken. Spoon into a bowl and chill in the refrigerator.

Whip the cream with the remaining sugar and vanilla and fold into the chilled zabaglione. Spoon over the pears and serve at once.

Trentino,	**PEACHES AND CREAM**	Serves 6
Alto Adige	*Pesche con la panna*	

This is a wonderfully refreshing dessert; the perfect ending to a filling meal. The original recipe uses all cream, but I prefer to use half yoghurt and half cream.

6 peaches
4 tablespoons Kirsch
6 teaspoons clear honey
50 g (2 oz) hazelnuts
350 ml (12 fl oz) plain yoghurt
350 ml (12 fl oz) single cream

Dip the peaches in boiling water for 1 minute. Remove the skins, cut in half and take out the stones. Slice the peaches and marinate in 3 tablespoons Kirsch mixed with 1 teaspoon honey for 30 minutes.

Spoon the peaches into individual glass dishes. Toast the hazelnuts in a preheated oven at 150°C (300°F/Gas Mark 3) for 30 minutes and then finely chop. Mix the yoghurt, cream and remaining honey and Kirsch together. Pour over the peaches and top with the toasted nuts. Serve at once.

All Italy   **CREAM CARAMEL**   Serves 4 to 6
Crema di caramello

Honey may be used as well as sugar to caramelize a mould. If using sugar, add 2 tablespoons water before bringing to the boil. Honey will take slightly longer than sugar to caramelize.

225g (8oz) clear honey or 100g (4oz) sugar
550ml (18fl oz) milk
3 eggs plus 2 egg yolks
1 teaspoon vanilla essence

Place about half the honey in a small, heavy-based saucepan and cook over a moderate heat for 4 to 5 minutes or until the honey darkens and starts to caramelize. Pour at once into a 900ml (1½ pint) mould or soufflé dish, tilting the dish in all directions until the caramel evenly lines the bottom and a little way up the sides of the mould. Set aside.

Scald the milk; do not let it boil or the custard will curdle. Remove from the heat and set aside to cool. Beat the eggs and egg yolks with the remaining honey until light. Gradually add the warm milk and vanilla essence. Pour through a fine sieve into the prepared mould.

Set the mould in a pan of hot water and place in the lower third of a preheated oven at 180°C (350°F/Gas Mark 4). Reduce the temperature to 160°C (325°F/Gas Mark 3) and bake for 40 to 45 minutes or until a knife comes out clean from the centre. Allow to cool to room temperature, then chill for several hours before unmoulding.

Piedmont   **CHOCOLATE ALMOND**   Serves 6
BAKED CUSTARD
Bonet

This is a delicious variation of cream caramel. If you prefer, 10 almonds, toasted in the oven at 180°C (350°F/ Gas Mark 4) and finely ground in the blender, may be substituted for the macaroons.

175g (6oz) sugar
2 tablespoons water
750ml (1¼ pints) milk
6 eggs
4 tablespoons cocoa or carob powder
2 tablespoons rum
50g (2oz) crushed amaretti

Place half the sugar in a small heavy based saucepan with 2 tablespoons water. Cook over a moderate heat for 4 to 5 minutes until the sugar starts to caramelize. Pour at once into a 1.5 litre (2½ pint) mould or soufflé dish, tilting the dish in all directions until the caramel evenly lines the bottom and sides of the mould. Set aside.

Scald the milk; do not let it boil or the custard will curdle. Remove from the heat and set aside to cool. Beat the eggs with the remaining sugar until light. Mix the warm milk with the cocoa powder in a blender until smooth, and gradually add to the egg mixture. Stir in the rum and the crushed macaroons. Pour into the prepared mould.

Set the mould in a pan of hot water and place in the lower third of a preheated oven at 180°C (350°F/Gas Mark 4). Reduce the heat to 160°C (325°F/Gas Mark 3) and bake for 40 to 45 minutes or until a knife comes out clean from the centre. Chill for several hours before unmoulding.

Campania **CHOCOLATE SEMIFREDDO** Serves 6
Semifreddo al cioccolato

Semifreddo means 'half cold'. It has the effect of tasting less cold than icecream, hence its name.

100g (4oz) ounces semi-sweet baking chocolate
4 tablespoons rum
2 cups heavy cream
6 tablespoons icing sugar
3 egg whites

Break the chocolate into squares and place in the top of a double-boiler over hot, not boiling, water. Add the rum and stir until the chocolate is melted and the mixture is smooth. Set aside to cool.

In a large mixing bowl, whip the cream with half of the sugar until it holds a shape, but not until it is stiff. In another bowl, beat the egg whites until stiff, then gradually beat in the remaining sugar. Lightly fold the chocolate mixture into the whipped cream, and then fold in the stiffly beaten egg whites. Do not handle any more than is necessary. Pour into a mold and freeze for at least 3 to 4 hours before serving.

Campania **ALMOND TORTONI** Serves 4
Tortoni di mandorle

500ml (16floz) double cream
40g (1½oz) icing sugar
2 tablespoons Amaretto liqueur
2 egg whites
50g (2oz) chopped toasted almonds

Whip the cream until it starts to thicken. Gradually add the sugar, beating constantly until the cream is stiff. Stir in the liqueur. Beat the egg whites until stiff and lightly fold into the cream and sugar mixture. Spoon it into individual paper cups and sprinkle each with toasted almonds. Freeze for 2 or 3 hours or until firm.

Campania	**PEAR SPUMONI**	Serves 4
	Spumoni di pere	to 6

6 pears
75g (3oz) sugar
120ml (4floz) dry white wine or water
50ml (2floz) brandy
350ml (12floz) double cream, whipped

Peel, core and slice the pears. Place them in a saucepan with the sugar and wine and simmer until the pears are soft and the wine has evaporated.

Pass the pears through a sieve, add the brandy and set aside to cool. Add the whipped cream and pour into a buttered charlotte mould. Cover with foil and freeze for 3 hours before serving.

INDEX